■ POSEIDON PRESS ■

New York London Toronto Sydney

Tokyo Singapore

Your
Family
Business

A Practical, Step-by-Step
Guide for Making Both
Your Relationships *and*
Your Business Rewarding
and Successful

Arthur Pine
WITH
JULIE HOUSTON

Poseidon Press
Simon & Schuster Building
Rockefeller Center
1230 Avenue of the Americas
New York, New York 10020

POSEIDON PRESS is a registered trademark
of Simon & Schuster Inc.

POSEIDON PRESS colophon is a trademark
of Simon & Schuster Inc.

Designed by Signet M Design, Inc.

Manufactured in the United States of America

10 9 8 7 6 5 4 3 2 1

Library of Congress Cataloging-in-Publication Data

Pine, Arthur.
    Your family business : a practical, step-by-step guide for making
both your relationships and your business rewarding and successful /
Arthur Pine with Julie Houston.
        p.   cm.
    1. Family corporations—Management.   I. Houston, Julie.
II. Title.
HD62.25.P56   1990
658'.045—dc20   90-7702
                                                                   CIP

ISBN 0-671-68986-X

To my family . . . my wife, Harriette (who knows why I love her) without whom we would not have two great sons, David and Richard, who brought into our family two beautiful and loving daughters-in-law, Dale and Nancy, and who, in turn, helped fill out our lives with four wonderful grandchildren, Ross, Alec, Adam and Gideon.

God bless them all for making my life such a joy.

Acknowledgments

I would like to thank Ann Patty for her courage and confidence that I could write this book—I never thought the day would come when I would be asked to do one. Special thanks go to Julie Houston, for all her assistance, and to Lori Andiman, for all her support; Lori has been a family member, though not by birth, for the last ten years. A word of appreciation to Marty Phillips, of Phillips Associates, family business consultants, and to Kathy Berliner for insights and encouragement.

Without a doubt, the lion's share of credit and thanks goes to the following firms and their family members for so generously taking time out from busy schedules to share their wisdom and thoughts—in sum total, representing an accumulated four generations and 160 successful years of family business experience:

Paul Bilsky, The Stephen Lawrence Company; Nello, John and Denise Botti, Designers Woodcraft; James Chin, Chin-Chin Restaurant; Frank Coussa, The American Pistachio Company; David Dalva, Dalva Brothers, Inc.; Sam and Karen Dorsky, The Dorsky Gallery; Arnold and Ilene Ferber, Pinpoint Marketing; Anne Dee and Leslie Goldin, Goldin Feldman Furs; Alan Greene, Buckingham Wax; Nathan, Aaron and Jeremiah Itzkowitz, The Yale Picture Frame

& Moulding Corporation; Drs. Herman and Sandy Katims; Alan, Bruce, Steve and Arnold Manheimer, J. Manheimer, Inc.; Peter Mosconi, Villa Mosconi Restaurant; Joanne and Jo Raimo, Joli Tours; Alan, Allyson and Carter Sackman, Sackman Enterprises, Inc.; Anthony Scicchitano and daughters Phyllis, Jo and Rita, The A & S Pork Store and The Small Feast Caterers; Howard, Jill and Jonathan Simon, Weston Equities; Irving and Jim Wallach, Wallach Sons of Manhasset, Inc. Jewelers; Leonard, Mark and Larry Wurzel, Calico Cottage Candies; Irwin and Linda Young, Du Art Film Laboratories.

So that comments could be given freely and candidly, the names of these contributors have been withheld throughout the text.

Contents

How This Book Came to Be Written

The primary audience for this book includes people involved with small and medium-sized businesses—businesses that employ up to 250 people and are owned by individual family members or a family group. However, I sincerely hope that those families who have larger firms will also find my philosophy to have a practical application to their own endeavors. Too often, a family business turns family members into enemies, instead of deepening the joy and satisfaction they should gain from working with one another.

When my publisher, Ann Patty, suggested that I write a book on the subject of family business because of the wonderful and successful relationship I have with my son, Richard, in our literary agency, I took the suggestion very lightly. After I realized that Ann was serious about the idea, I gave it more thought—especially since just the night before, my wife and I had been at a friend's house for dinner and one of the guests had asked what my secret was for having such a successful business relationship with my son. Unfortunately, this person's business relationship with his son had proven to be a failure. I asked the father, "In what position did you start your son when he came into the business after graduating college?" He answered, "I started him just like I did—loading cartons on the truck." That was his first mistake. I explained that today's young men and women can learn how to load cartons on a truck (if that is necessary at all) *after* they are actively engaged in the business. His thinking was old-fashioned. I told him that when Richard joined the agency, I treated him as my equal right from the start. I wanted him to know that he was respected, needed and wanted. After talking to this dinner guest, I began to realize that too many family businesses are not successful because the senior members have the wrong attitude about how to indoctrinate and train younger family members when they join the business, and how to work with them as time goes by.

I was fortunate to know Julie Houston and to have her work with me on this book. Together we interviewed more than one hundred members of family businesses in various fields to get their insights on how they made their businesses successful (and, in some cases, not so successful). This book will give you useful tips and advice on how you too can have a happy and successful family business that will enrich your life.

How My Business Became a Family Business

"**B**ring Richard into the business? That's the last thing I can picture ever working out. I give it four days of working together before both of you change your minds. Four days."

That was my wife speaking, fourteen years ago, when I told her of my plan to offer our son a job in my literary agency. And looking back over the odds, I have to admit the safe bet on whether Richard and I could make a go of it was clearly in her corner. The idea of our working together came up so unexpectedly that even I suspected her assessment might be right.

During his sophomore year at the University of Pennsylvania, Richard came home on his spring break agonizing over what to do with his life. It was time to declare his major for the next two years, and he was in turmoil about it. "I don't want to be a doctor," he said. "I don't want to be a CPA or a lawyer. I don't want to go to graduate school. I'm spending a substantial amount of your money on tuition, and I don't even know what I want to be."

"Richard," I said, trying to calm him down, "at the age of nineteen you don't have to worry about what you want to do for the rest of your life, what field to choose. Just having an education will always come in handy."

Giving Richard reassurance started me thinking more about his situation, and a few days later when I was getting ready for work, I called him in to propose a plan. "What about the possibility of coming into the office this summer to see whether you might like it?" I asked. I thought he just might like it, because from the time he first learned to read, Richard had devoured everything he could get his hands on—from comic books to the classics to contemporary literature. Perhaps being a literary agent was his true vocation, I thought.

Richard said he hadn't really considered coming into business with me, but that he would think about it.

We didn't talk about it again during his vacation, but about a month later, after he was back at school, he called me.

"I've been thinking about that summer job you offered me, Dad," he said. "If you're still game, I'd like to try it out."

And so it happened, fourteen years ago, that Richard first arrived to work in my office and the business was on the way to becoming a family business.

Now, Richard and I couldn't have been a more unlikely pair to team up in an office. He'd always had a mind of his own, and I didn't know if he would be able to listen and learn as he went along. I didn't even know if he'd like to work in an office at all—his previous summer jobs consisted of scrubbing down boats or working as a camp counselor, and he seemed to gravitate naturally to working outdoors. However, I felt confident that we could make it work because I had great respect for his mind, his character and his love of literature. I thought he might fit into the business very well.

And he did. Working together in adjacent offices, our business has evolved into one of the more successful literary agencies in all of publishing, representing such clients as Dr. Wayne Dyer, George Burns, Bob Hope, Dr. Martin Katahn and Katherine Dunn, among about one hundred others. In the publishing industry, our father-son connection is a very visible one, and not a day passes that somebody doesn't ask me how we've managed to work so well together and for so long. Parents who are thinking about bringing their children into business constantly ask for my secrets for success, and I get wistful reactions from families who have tried to work together and failed.

To be honest, Richard and I really don't have any secrets for staying together. The key for us was simply that I really wanted it to work—I was determined deep down in my gut to *make* it work. That was the bottom line. Moreover, from day one, Richard wanted it to work. He loved the world of publishing as much as I did—the excitement of finding great new book properties and selling them to top publishers; the satisfaction of building close personal connections with our authors; the negotiating of subsidiary-rights deals with people in the publishing, film and television business, here and abroad.

Were there conflicts? Of course there were. To this day, we still have our differences. Nevertheless, together we have managed to feel our way along the same bumpy, winding road every family member in business must negotiate if he or she is going to make the working relationship a success. We've grappled with the challenges—getting through the entry process and early days when Richard was as green in the business as they come, handling mistakes, keeping our clients happy, dealing with editors and publishers, managing money matters, and so forth.

Along the way, we found ways to shape our working relationship, resolve our differences and work together as a team. And if there is any underlying secret to our success, it is the desire to keep our relationship thriving, and never losing sight of that desire. It's not all that difficult if you really want it. As you will see in the chapters that follow, other families may handle their relationships differently than we do, but I haven't met one family who is succeeding in business together who doesn't operate on that basic premise.

With this book as a resource, I am convinced that any family that really wants to work together in business—establishing compatible motives to do so and putting honest efforts into building a solid, productive working relationship—can make it happen. Richard and I—along with the many parents, offspring, brothers, sisters, cousins, aunts and uncles interviewed for this book—are family business people with strengths and weaknesses just like yours. We have all made our way through the vulnerable areas in a family business—basic training, handling mistakes, spending money, expanding the business, working with nonfamily members, bringing in siblings, planning succession and all the other "hot spots" where emotions can intrude. As you will discover, there is no pat formula for protecting personal relationships from being harmed or destroyed in a family business; everyone has his or her own way of dealing with such potential problems. As you will also discover, it is this wonderful diversity of personalities and experiences that provides the greatest resource for finding your own special route to success. Picking and choosing from the strategies, tips and skills shared by others in the chapters that follow, you have every chance of shaping the most solid, productive working relationship you could ever hope for in a family business.

Part One

Preentry

1 Is Working Together Really Worth the Risk?

Starting with examples of how family members decide to work together in business, this chapter explores the positive side of that decision. If by the end of the chapter, you can't convince yourself that you really want to work with your family, you would probably be better off not even considering teaming up with them. But with the desire and commitment to give it a shot, along with this book as your guide, you are already well on your way to making the business relationship with your family a success.

Of course, timing is critical. Richard and I were lucky because both of us came to our decision to try working together at about the same time. Other families have to do more groundwork to prepare for teaming up together. Yet once the decision to work together becomes mutual, other families have no less chance for succeeding than we did.

As for how families arrive at the point of mutual willingness, let's look at some of the variables to see how often they involve timing, planning and, sometimes, persistence and patience.

Example I: One family member wants to bring in others who are reluctant or, as is more often the case, resisting.

The classic, very common situation is that parents want their children or other relatives to join the business, but they aren't yet ready to.

After many years, one art-gallery owner realized that he "really had something" in terms of the acquisitions and knowledge he'd amassed over the years, and rather than let it all slip into some stranger's hands, he wanted to pass the business along to his family. He approached his daughter with the idea. "As he encouraged, I resisted," she describes, "to the point where I said, 'If you bring it up again, I'm not even going to come see you.' "

In situations like this, it is *always* up to the child to decide about coming in; this father had no choice but to wait patiently and accept whatever decision his daughter would make. After teaching in Paris, she did in fact change her mind. She had been fighting with her father for so long, she finally said to herself, "This is stupid. He's not getting any younger and if I am going to see the business at all, I may as well see it now, while he's still so active in it." And in she came—ready, willing and able to learn all she could from her father, whose patience and persistence finally won out. In fact, this daughter was wise in her thinking. One son whose father died suddenly of a heart attack realized the family business was where he wanted to be—intensely wanted to be—to carry on all his father's hard work. He's doing so now but wishing he'd started much earlier, when his father was around to coach and encourage him.

Knowing their parents really want them in the business, many children will indeed change their minds and come in—provided, once again, they are given the choice. One father very patiently stood by as his daughter pursued graduate courses in accounting, working toward a CPA degree; at one point he offered her the chance to travel in Spain, become fluent in Spanish and then work at the family's television station in Puerto Rico. At first, she turned down his offer, but it was not too long afterward that she realized the path she had chosen for herself was not something she could enjoy as a career—and once again, her father made his proposal. This time she took him up on it, became an expert in the language, gained thirteen months' valuable experience traveling on her own and returned eager to work with her father. Now, after six years, she is poised to take over leadership as the third generation in this family's business.

In some cases, a parent's desire to bring a child into the business comes up urgently and unexpectedly. One father who owned both a successful advertising agency and a foundering marketing company made an eleventh-hour decision to try to keep the marketing business alive—but he also decided he needed his levelheaded, reliable and trustworthy daughter, who was a potter at the time, to work at it with him. "I'm a terrific salesman and I worked her over pretty well," this father explained, "only to have her say no." He persisted, however, and finally she agreed to a one-year trial period at resuscitating the stripped-down-to-the-bones company. Twelve years later, with the marketing firm thriving and their father-daughter business relationship more solid than ever, they look back and joke about her initial reluctance to join the business. Now proud of their accomplishments, this twosome had no idea things would work out so well, but parental persistence in an urgent situation ultimately paid off in a big way for both of them.

In another family, two brothers were *very* patient about

waiting for the possibility of their sons taking over the family jewelry business. They paved the way for a smooth succession far in advance by splitting the business in half—dividing their assets and inventory equally—and setting up businesses on their own in different locations. Twenty years passed before either of their sons showed a trace of interest in the business, but when ultimately each of them came in with his respective parent, everything was in place for him, and thus the brothers' planning was finally rewarded.

Example 2: The younger generation wants to come in, but the parents try to discourage it.

If a son or daughter shows interest in wanting to join the business, you don't know how lucky you are. Don't discourage it. Give it a chance.

Sometimes parents will try to persuade their children to do something else for a living because they think the family business is just too hard or too risky, as was the case with one son whose mother and father urged him to stay out of the family business and work for some big firm like IBM. "They didn't encourage me because I think ultimately they felt that the business was never going to make it," the son explains, "and that it would never get as big as it is. My mother still wonders about its success."

What did this son do? He went out and got the kind of corporate job that made his parents happy, and then he brought back into the family firm all the new skills he had learned, increasing profits tremendously. He persuaded his parents to let him in, proved his worth and watched the business thrive because of it.

For one reason or another, some parents view their children as a risk. This was the case when a son borrowed money from his parents to start up a music-promotion business that eventually went bankrupt. Afterward, the father held on to the image of his son as a failure, even though the experience had taught the son a valuable lesson about business. It took many years of convincing before the father finally agreed to let his son come into the business.

Then there is the age-old issue of sex stereotyping. Until recently, some businesses were considered so exclusively male-oriented that daughters were encouraged to stay out. This attitude has changed, as demonstrated most notably by Hugh Hefner's turning over *Playboy* magazine to his daughter, but many young women can still point to its influence on their career decisions.

In a family business that was traditionally run by "little gray-haired men," one daughter didn't even think of bringing up the subject of working with her father, but instead got an outside job in merchandising. She was rapidly promoted to executive status, and when her father saw how good she was, he thought to himself, "Why take all that talent elsewhere? I want her in here with me!"

Timing was doubly in their favor because as he was wooing her in, the industry was rapidly opening up to women. Their decision to work together provided a great opportunity for both of them. She's the first woman in four generations to run the company and is doing so with enormous success.

As these examples show, when children are willing and eager to come into the business, it pays to keep an open mind about welcoming them in. However, you've also got to trust your instincts. You know your own children pretty well, and at the time they may want to come in, you may be in a better position to judge whether they are ready or even if they are good candidates at all. In fact, I know one father who felt that his son was not well suited for his ad agency, and when the topic came up, he had no qualms about putting his arm around his son and encouraging him to pursue his own thing. With some disappointment but no hard feelings, the son went off and did just that, and several years later, seeing that there was indeed a place for his now mature and very talented son, the father approached him with an offer of a position in the company. This time, it was the son's turn to put his arm around his father and to turn down the offer.

"I went home and sucked my thumb for a while," says the father, all the while understanding the decision and to this day extremely proud of his son's enormous success elsewhere.

Example 3: Both parties start out with the desire to work together, but ultimately fail.

The typical case is that of family members who get along wonderfully—until they get into an office together.

"This was going to be the greatest team going," reflects one father. "My daughter and I were really going to knock them dead, we were going to improve the business, we were going to make it big—and instead we fell on our faces."

Lack of planning was this father's downfall. Like others whose children never progress beyond the entry stage, he hadn't taken the time to think through his own expectations and priorities. It took a whole year of not speaking to each other, waiting for their anger to cool, for this father-daughter team to begin rebuilding the valued personal relationship they lost. They have not even tried to regain the professional one—at least not yet.

Unfortunately, it is often families who have failed at working together who provide the most valuable lessons in how to keep relationships intact in a family business. In the above case, while there was mutual willingness to give it a try, the father jumped into their new relationship demanding far more of his daughter than he would have demanded of other employees—perfection was not good enough. His attitude was entirely unrealistic. You should expect from your child what you expect from others—nothing more or less.

As for why he imposed such an unrealistic standard of perfection, this gentleman admits it was in reaction to a certain unexpected jealousy he felt when he discovered that in his absence his daughter ran the show better than he did. If that happens, great! It's what you should hope and strive for, paving the way as soon as your child joins the firm—without showing any outward preference over nonfamily employees and others—by encouraging others with whom you work to have as much respect for your child as they do for you.

This scenario points up the importance of thinking your own situation through very carefully, and if necessary doing some soul-searching and reshaping basic attitudes and aspirations about one of the biggest long-term investments you'll ever make—bringing in and training family for leadership roles in the family business.

Example 4: The decision to work together is never discussed; it merely happens.

When family members seem to slip easily into the place carved out for them in the business, some families point to what I call "the osmosis factor." In the words of one father, "I never pictured bringing my sons in; it just happened." The osmosis factor just seems to condition those who have lived and breathed the family business since birth to the prospect of making a career out of it.

Pointing to an old sepia photograph on her desk, one daughter explains how the business "goes back to the prehistoric ages"; how she and her sister are "purebred fur people," third generation on both sides of the family and proud of it. An art and antiques dealer describes how, as children, he and his brothers were constantly hearing conversations about the family business—while also living across the street from the Metropolitan Museum of Art in New York, where they often saw fine antiques similar to those they now buy and sell. Now he's bringing in his son—the newest, fourth generation member of the family business.

Many children who come into their parents' business with enthusiasm and pride often credit the osmosis factor for giving them a surprisingly smooth entry. "Some people can go into the kitchen and whip up a meal; when I came into my father's business, I found being there just came naturally to me," one daughter discovered to her delight. Absorbing the business into their system from the time they are born, such children naturally love it.

Others, however, try to escape "their destiny" like the plague. "My greatest fear was that others would look at me and say that I went into the family business because I couldn't make it on my own . . . that I wasn't sharp enough to make my own living elsewhere," confesses the son in a family jewelry business.

After proving himself by "doing his own thing" successfully elsewhere, this young man came into his parent's business with new confidence, receptive and ready to excel in the very challenging job of managing the business.

As his situation and those of the other families mentioned here illustrate, no one can be forced into doing something he or she doesn't want to do. In many situations, however, encouragement from the parent can be extremely effective in reinforcing motivation to join and stay in the family business. Children often don't see the long-term benefits of working together when they are young and new to a business; they tend to look at the here and now. It doesn't hurt to tell them often how fortunate you as a parent feel to have them on board, pointing out that while the possibilities of working elsewhere for more money may seem appealing in the short run, in the long run the children will be much better off financially and much more secure if they stick with the family business.

SIX WAYS TO HARNESS THE OSMOSIS FACTOR

Parents who recognize early on that they want their children to join the business can use the following guidelines to help promote a positive attitude about it:

■ <u>Talk about the family business.</u>

Let your children know it's an important part of your life that you want to share with your family. Let them see how "hooked" you are on your work so that they will have a model of job commitment to emulate.

■ <u>Give children ways to feel proud of what you do in the business.</u>

It's never too early to share your accomplishments—and those of past generations in the business, if applicable— with your children. Each year, one father arranges for his son's school classes to tour the family business—the highlight of the year for his proud son.

■ Give children ways to feel proud of what they can do.

One father in the fudge-mix business brings his two youngsters into the office on weekends. While he works on the computer, they feed envelopes into the mailing machine and catch them at the other end. "They're ready to quit kindergarten right now and come into the business," jokes their father, knowing he's sown the first seeds of work enjoyment.

Another father often takes his son on business trips during high-school vacations. Not only are such times special, as father and son spend time together, but the son also provides valuable assistance setting up merchandise for sales presentations.

■ Balance bad news about work with good news.

If the nightmares are all that they hear about, you can be sure your children will gravitate to anything *but* the family business. Tell them what turns you on at work—bring home news of what's fun, what makes you feel good about the business. If the children do end up coming in, let them learn about the negative aspects later as they go along.

In my particular case, I enjoy my business so much that Richard has heard me tell people over and over again that I can't wait to get into the office in the morning because every day brings something new and exciting. Of course, I am very fortunate to be in such a business. Now Richard feels the same way.

■ Keep career choices open so that children
feel comfortable discussing future plans—
whether these include coming into the business
or not.

When Richard was in a quandary about what career to pursue, I doubt he would have thought about coming into the
agency. I didn't avoid the subject; I wanted him to know
the door was open. In his case, he chose to walk in.

At the same time, you must be ready to accept whatever
career path your child decides to follow. "If my son is interested in the business, the time will come when he'll tell
us," explains one father. "And if he doesn't want to join the
business, he can tell me right up front. He doesn't have to
have the business."

■ Never push.

Family members will be off and running if you pressure
them to work with you—they'll feel it's expected. Let
them see for themselves the merits of being in one's own
business. "My daughters saw what the business could do
for our family—how nicely we could live," observes one
father, "and how the business also gives you a sense of
freedom. You are free when you've got your own business.
If you want to sit, you sit. You want to get up, you get
up. You want to work hard to increase the business, you
work. You want to take a day off, you have no one to
ask for permission." These are some of the advantages
that his children recognized and that lured them into the
business.

ADVANTAGES OF A SUCCESSFUL
PROFESSIONAL RELATIONSHIP

Let's jump ahead for a moment and look at some of the positive things that can happen when you make a success of the professional relationship with your family—rewards that are not only deeply personal but, more often than not, also highly profitable. A harmonious working relationship will have many positive effects on your business.

■ **It brings new blood and new energy into the business.**

After working for fifty years in his own jewelry business, one father put it very well when describing the positive effect of his son's arrival on the scene. "Your thinking—*my* thinking—gets very stilted," he said. "I'm too involved with the way the business was when I began. Everything is different now. I'm finding it difficult to make the transfer, to take in the new concepts, but to my son it's a new business."

When family members come in with a fresh, positive attitude, it's contagious. "The thing I like about having my children here is their enthusiasm," explains another father. "They get you charged up. It's good to go into a meeting when they're saying, 'Let's go get 'em, Dad.' They get you pumped up because they have a lot of ideas. Some are a little on the wild side, but at least it gets you thinking."

"At this stage of my life," explains another parent, "I don't need it anymore; I've done it all. I get a kick out of making deals, but after that I lose interest." With his children now in the picture, this father enjoys making the deals, while his kids are happy to learn the business by handling the follow-up.

I can personally attest to the fact that the younger generation thinks and does things with more guts than their parents' generation. When Richard makes a deal for an author, he will often ask a publisher for double or triple the amount of money I would ask for. If it were me, I would sit down and think it out and figure how much of a gamble the particular book might be for the publisher, putting myself in his or her shoes to assess how much I would pay for it. Richard, on the other hand, puts himself in the authors' shoes, thinking how their hard work deserves absolutely the most money that can be gotten from a publisher. Not only does he succeed most of the time in getting what he thinks the book is worth but more often than not, his assessment proves to be uncannily accurate because the book usually turns out to be a very big seller and a profitmaker for all concerned.

■ <u>It makes the business more productive.</u>

Ask families how much time they spend at their business and usually the answer from those who are running the show is in the range of "three hundred and sixty-five days a year." That's why sharing management with family can be so appealing. Says one father, "A lot of people walk out of here at five, five-thirty, but I know the kids are going to stay here and be interested, and be thinking business at the dinner table and the next day and on Saturdays and Sundays."

Whatever the investment in time, when family is working together there's an even greater chance for increasing productivity. "It's better to work for your family than to work for strangers," sums up one business owner. "You work harder."

Working in her father's real-estate office with two brothers and an uncle, another young woman further explains why she and her siblings are so productive. "You are always striving for your parents' approval either in business or at home," she says. "And sometimes when you ordinarily wouldn't be doing something—maybe because it's dedication to the business or to your parents—you go the extra ten yards."

When parents allow their children to do what they do best, and encourage them to seek a high level of performance, the business will benefit and so will the child. "Because he gives us such freedom in here," says one daughter of her father's attitude, "there really are boundless opportunities to create and expand. The work remains ever challenging."

"What he lets you do," explains another daughter who is also working with her father in business, "is pursue certain goals in your own style; he gives you an incredible amount of freedom. And it's kind of a double-edged sword in a way, because you're really out there."

This is one individual who is surely gaining confidence in creating her own niche and leadership style and, to my mind, her father is very smart. Giving children freedom to do as they please, and assuring them that if they make a mistake the business is not going to fold, is one of the best ways to encourage them to make their own decisions and take on responsibility.

■ It supports life stages in a special way.

One of the biggest challenges to businesses today is accommodating the special needs of executives involved in early parenting. In such situations, family businesses can be especially supportive. Explains one woman executive, "I cram as much into three days as I did in five. Everyone knows it, but I doubt any other business would care to accommodate my schedule, or to accept it."

"This is the nicest time of all to work for family rather than for anyone else," says one new mother. "They really want me to put my baby first, and I can come back in whenever I feel ready." In the presence of an energetic team of family members, there's less chance of a lag in productivity—her family may happily do double duty, if need be, to make up for this woman's taking time off to be with her baby.

Support from family does not just involve caring for children. For members of the older generation, knowing that they can eventually turn over certain responsibilities of business to eager children adds a special measure of support, to say nothing of job security. Elsewhere, they might be thrown out with a forced retirement. This is particularly true in businesses in which the physical aspects of the job may become a challenge, or when a reduced workload becomes necessary. Working with family also helps in maintaining a positive attitude toward coming in to work at all. After thirty years or so of being the only family member in the office, one father/boss comments, "Working with my daughter, I've learned that I like having family around. It's kind of a meaningful thing coming to work. At this stage of my life, I like it. It's given me a desire to keep this business going."

In another situation, as the years went by, the father found he depended more and more on his daughter. "Because of her maturity," he says, "and the longevity of our relationship, and also because of where I'm at, I lean on her a lot more. We've had a couple of real crises this week involving a second business that we have, and she's not only my sounding board, she's also my adviser. She's the one I would go to first. She's a true partner in every sense of the word. I don't think of it as father-daughter in a business sense."

■ It attracts new business and new clients.

Either out of lack of interest, motivation or awareness, some members of the older generation ignore areas that could generate more business—until younger family members come in. "I was brought up in a well-to-do house where there was an old-fashioned concept that money was considered offensive," explains one father candidly, "and I feel that my daughter is much better at business than I am. She's got her mother's instincts." In this situation, the daughter apparently benefits not only from being one generation removed from her father's attitude about money, but also from growing up being influenced by certain attitudes of her mother who, according to the father, "didn't want her daughters to be dependent upon men for anything."

"My daughter has a very good handle on advertising," the founder of a prestigious art gallery explains. "She knows how to get publicity for the gallery, which is something I never paid attention to because I'd always been uncomfortable about it."

Parents who recognize their children as assets in attracting new business rave at the results. As one media advertiser candidly puts it, "My son has made a contribution over the last five years that has changed the face of this agency. He has attracted clients who are bigger. He has attracted talent I could not have brought in."

For the very same reasons this gentleman describes, I too can rave about my son's contributions to our business. Richard has brought a new dimension to our client list that I had never actively pursued, which evolved not only because of our age difference, but also because of our own backgrounds and interests. My background is in business; I see the commercial potential of a manuscript, first and foremost, and if I think it will sell, I will send it out to a publisher. Richard, however, has his own standards. The book may be commercial, but it also has to have a certain literary quality if his name is to be associated with it. You might think this would lead to problems, but, in fact, it has done just the opposite. Nothing gives me more pleasure than to see how Richard's standards have started to pay off for our business.

One recent book stands out as a good example. After reading the manuscript for *Geek Love*, by Katherine Dunn, Richard came running into the office and said, "Dad, Katherine Dunn is a genius. This is a piece of literature that will live for years."

Now, if I had been the only one in the office and had read the book cold, I surely would have seen the author's great literary talents, but I doubt whether I would have been as excited about the manuscript, because the story is a most unusual one and I would probably have wondered about its commercial possibilities. But Richard's instincts proved to be absolutely right. He arranged to have it published by Alfred A. Knopf, Inc., one of the most prestigious publishers in the United States, and in 1989 the book was nominated for the National Book Award.

Richard's continued ability to attract new clients who have a more literary quality to their work than the good, solid authors whom I had previously represented has really benefited the agency. His ability has helped us expand and be recognized as handling not only extremely commercial books, but highly literary works as well.

One mother shared her view of her daughter's being an asset in attracting business. "I learned from working with my daughter that she is much more outgoing than I am, and she is wonderful when we are going after new clientele. She can walk into an office and set a whole scene. She relaxes everybody. And then if I have a little more knowledge, I may come on and use it. She opens the doors, and then I come in."

■ **It helps ensure continuity, stability and the trust of outsiders.**

Reliability—longevity and endurance in the form of a healthy, multigeneration family business—is a valuable financial asset that instills trust inside and outside the office. It helps to keep clients and customers coming back, and it helps to attract new money from banks and investors when the time comes for the business to grow. For this reason, parents who pave the way early for their children to come in—letting them know it's a good place to work and giving them a chance to pitch in—sow the seeds for the business's healthy future.

"They have heard conversations around the table since they were five years old," says one father who grew up listening to his own parents share their hopes and dreams for the business; now his children are proud to be part of the team.

The idea of family continuity in business may be a parent's dream, but sometimes it is a dream that even they don't recognize right away. One father who had never considered his children coming in—wasn't for it or against it, but just never discussed it—realized only after grooming outsiders to take over that he was uncomfortable turning his life's efforts and success over to strangers. When his two daughters unexpectedly expressed interest in coming in, he welcomed them with open arms.

■ It sets a model of stability for other employees, fostering long-term interest and loyalty to the business.

In a time of corporate takeovers and consolidation in business—coupled with a high level of distrust of certain politicians, religious leaders and businessmen—a solid family business promotes a rare base of security among nonfamily employees.

"We feel that with all this merger mania and leveraged buyouts people want to feel secure," explains one fourth-generation family executive. "When there's that kind of conflict going on, people are very insecure because they don't know what tomorrow will bring. And many times, the corporate office may be thousands of miles away and they never even meet the boss. Here, if you've got a problem, you can come in to see any of us in the family, discuss it and chances are it gets resolved quickly, keeping tension levels to a minimum."

Some family businesses have such a solid reputation for their stability that nonfamily members bring in their own family—a practice that might be frowned on elsewhere but which is no problem when a family is receptive to the idea that talent for a certain kind of work might run in a family. "We have brothers and sisters, husbands and wives," brags one young executive in his family business. "Some are even in the same department!"

Of course, no matter who comes into the business—relatives of nonfamily employees or your own children—the key is that they have a feel for it. Giving them the freedom to nurture their own particular interests will often help determine their profession, as was the case with my two sons, Richard and David. Richard was always the avid reader, while David, who was smart and did well at school, had other interests. He is now a very successful doctor of chiropractics in Pompano Beach, Florida, and I don't think I ever would have encouraged him to come into the agency.

The loyalty to nonfamily stems directly from the family values at the heart of the family business. Says one executive, "We don't have five families to feed [referring to the families headed by his relatives who are working together]; we have a hundred and thirty families [referring to the dependents of nonfamily employees]. If things are bad," he adds, "nonfamily employees come first."

Nonfamily workers benefit indirectly from the harmonious relationships between the parent/boss and his or her children, which often improves day-to-day communication between the boss and other employees. "Coming into work is a special pleasure," says one parent/boss. "I'm more relaxed with them around; it's a more relaxed and fun place to be for everyone."

■ It strengthens family ties.

When work opportunities pull family members from one location and resettle them elsewhere, roots can be lost in just one generation. In this age of transience, those family members who are working happily together in business value their close connections.

I love seeing Richard every day, and as for the closeness being a challenge, I agree with the restaurateur who dismisses it. "I don't look at it as a challenge," he says. "I look on it as a pleasure because with everything being so busy—rush, rush, the rat race—you never get a chance to spend time with your family. We're so lucky to be able to work together."

The office, or place of business, can become a special

kind of family meeting ground. "There's just a lot of ca-maraderie," one son sums it up. "For me," says a daughter about her work, "I feel as if I have two homes, and this is one of them."

"Sure there is an element of risk, but you also have a chance of making it better," one son comments on the work-ing relationship with his father. "Not only better, but getting to know each other as one adult to another."

Of our own working relationship, Richard comments, "Had I not come in to work with my dad, I probably would have missed a chance ever to get to really know him. We were in the same house when I was growing up, but we shared very few interests. We liked each other, but the bonding just wasn't there. I think that behind our getting together—his wanting me in the agency and my being at-tracted to working in it—there was an unspoken, uncon-scious curiosity about each other. And if there is a drawback to seeing my father every day, it is that we don't get together much in our free time and thus I don't see enough of my mother, the parent I did have a bond with all during the time I was growing up."

Many families readily comment on how working together creates a unique bond of understanding.

"For me and my father," explains one son, "working to-gether has created a closeness between us because it's some-thing he can talk about with me."

"I realized my father counts on me more than he counts on anyone," states one daughter. "I'm not an employee! We're a team. We all [including her brothers] operate as a team."

"We've become grown-up friends first, a whole new thing," says one father of his two boys. "They're a lot of fun to be around."

"He really needs us here," two children have discovered about their father. "He really cares about me; I never really knew that," says another.

"It's a new relationship for us both," says one young man. "He tries to be my mentor and actually he does a good job of it."

"He gives me my freedom," says one daughter. "I really feel he respects my opinion and he's not afraid to have me fail. He wants me to learn that way."

In a working relationship, individuals often recognize and develop a deeper appreciation of the values they share as a family. "I've learned a tremendous amount about my father by working with him in business," explains one daughter. "I see him as my mentor as well as my father. And he's very capable." To which her father reacted with delight, "You never said that before!"

Through the working relationship, family values often come to light, with a deeper appreciation for them.

"Watching him do business, I see that my father is the most generous and probably the fairest person I've met in my life. And the most honest."

"I can see that through my parents, we all have our morals in the right place. When you're finished arguing and the smoke clears, that's what shines through and what really matters," comments one daughter. "We're all fighting for the same thing," her father adds, while her brother exclaims, "It's nothing like *Dynasty!*"

Reviewing the pluses, is it worth risking family harmony to work in business together? From those of us who are making it succeed, the answer is definitely yes.

Is it worth *your* taking the risk? If the desire to give it a go is mutual, it's certainly worth a try. The unlikeliest matches have been known to succeed, even those involving parents and children who have been at odds all their lives. Many even find new ways to resolve or leave behind old conflicts and end up thriving together at work.

I believe that Richard's and my greatest asset was wanting to make our working relationship succeed, coupled with my decision right from the start to make him my equal in the agency, not only in my mind, but in the eyes of our business associates, authors and publishers alike. In the chapters that follow, you will find many details of our personal experiences in making a success of our business relationship, but we are only one situation, and many other, very different families have contributed their own ideas for working together happily and efficiently.

2 Making It a Family Business: Are You Suited for Success?

After Richard called me from college with his decision to work in the office, a curious thing happened to him during the rest of his sophomore year. He worked less, but his grades got better. He was happier—as he describes it, he was soaring. The prospect of becoming a literary agent changed his whole life, he says, because suddenly he felt he knew who he was.

To this day, Richard asserts that coming into the agency was the opportunity of a lifetime. It literally gave him the chance to get a ten-year jump on a career, at a time when his college friends were floating around wondering who they were, what they were going to do with their lives and how they were going to do it. Incoming members in other family businesses often agree with Richard's assessment. Arriving on the scene in a well-established business run by family gives them a big jump on applying their talents and making a success out of their work.

When Richard was in a quandary about his life, he was feeling the pressure to compete in a world that every day becomes more competitive. If you employ your children, the one great gift you are giving them is the gift of time— a period of security during which they can learn and excel without having to struggle needlessly to find their niche. It's not a question of being afraid to compete. Certain competition is counterproductive; knowing when the pressure is getting the best of you is one of the most important lessons to learn about yourself throughout life. Thankfully, Richard seemed to have this intuitive ability ever since his early days in school.

If an incoming family member is candid enough to tell the world that joining the family business is the path of least resistance and, given the opportunity, is ready, willing and eager to learn and flourish—great! It not only shows a willingness to seize the opportunity offered, but also to capitalize on that opportunity.

Nepotism? Not really. If children are to succeed, they will have to prove their worth through the quality of their work—not by being the boss's sons or daughters. Moreover, even if some of them never turn out to be managers, at least they will have found that out without getting knifed in the back.

Richard and I were lucky to have a good relationship to begin with; it was not an issue when we became working partners. What was more significant is that by the time he came in for that first summer job, I had already thought through the whole situation and knew exactly how I was going to approach our working relationship: *I was going to make him an equal partner.*

I was not going to start him off as the office boy, or delivering packages or doing the kind of clerical work that could easily be done by someone else. Rather, I was going to set him up in a office of equal size right next to mine and, until he got the hang of the job, Richard would be my shadow. I knew that he was much, much smarter than I had been at his age, and I was confident that the skills he might miss by not working his way up through the ranks he would pick up along the way.

This was my basic approach, and it succeeded for a number of reasons. For example, the layout of space was perfect for setting up adjacent offices so that Richard could be directly involved. Because much of our business is done by telephone, Richard was privy to the basics without making outsiders feel uneasy about it. When I knew I was going to have an important conversation with a publisher or an author that I felt would be advantageous for Richard to hear, I would signal him to pick up his phone and listen in. In that way, he was actually getting a lesson in business. He was learning, simply by listening, the skills of how to negotiate, how to handle people, how to be an agent.

Other parents describe taking quite a different tack—it all depends on the nature of the job and the kind of work you are in. Some parents/bosses call on their middle management people to steer the children through an early training period. Some children/trainees are more comfortable working behind the scenes at first, for example, filling out orders. That way, they build up confidence as they learn the mechanics of the business without being immediately on the front line. Others prefer to dive right in, sink or swim, knowing they have an encouraging parent in the wing for support.

In each case, the key is finding an approach that makes you comfortable. And how do you do this? One good way is to begin asking yourself the following questions, which can reveal how well suited you are, by temperament and by motive, for working in a family business. Use your answers to help tailor your own best approach to a compatible, productive working relationship and, if necessary, improve or eliminate certain behavior traits that could work against it.

SEVEN QUESTIONS FOR THE PARENTS

Question 1: Do I see our teaming up together not as an obligation, but an opportunity?

If you feel that your children owe you, forget it. If you feel that by getting them into the business, you can get out of something you don't like that much sooner—forget that too. "I told them not to come in," states one father. "I said, 'Look, don't do me any favors.' Because if you make your kids come into the business, they won't stay. If they want to come in and they love the work, they will learn, they will stay."

The casualty stories are many. One third-generation family member describes the anxiety he felt when it was "his time" to come into the business—his grandfather had forced it on his father, his father expected it of him, and since no one really liked what he was doing in the first place, everyone fought about everything. In such a situation, where each generation expects the next one to get him off the hook, the business was doomed by the third generation—indeed, in this case, when the person refused to come in, there was a terrible, angry upheaval, and the business folded.

To bring in family, you yourself have got to honestly love your business—truly believe that it has real potential and that it presents rich, enjoyable and good career opportunities for your children.

If it's seen as an opportunity for incoming members of the family to join the business, it should also be seen as an opportunity for the parent/boss. The owner of a highly successful business handling commercial real estate describes how the prospect of bringing his children in gave him the opportunity to view his life from a whole new perspective.

Rather than spend 100 percent of his time on business, he was going to work only 50 percent of the time, have a ball traveling and enjoying his leisure time 25 percent of the time, and devote the remaining 25 percent to charity and volunteer work in his community. He created a rare opportunity for himself to create a balance in his life, and is that much happier for it.

When I suggested to my son, Richard, that he might come into the business, my primary thought was that it was a good business and that it was something that seemed to be made to order for him because of his love of books and his love for people in general—publishing is the kind of business where you work one-on-one much of the time. As for the advantages to me of having him come in, I didn't really realize at first how much easier business would become with him involved and how much spare time I could eventually have, if I wanted it. However, as Richard became more and more experienced, I realized that I could take off two weeks at a time instead of one, or even a month and not worry one bit about how the business was going. By nature I am a workaholic and happy to admit it, and when I am away I have complete confidence in Richard. And the fun part of it is, if we should get ten calls in the office in an hour, seven of them are for Richard and three are for me. This is the ideal situation that I eventually came to hope for.

Question 2: Am I really ready to loosen my hold on the business?

If I planned to make Richard my equal, other parents are prepared to go even further—reversing roles so they work for their offspring.

"I may disagree with him here and there, but it never comes to blows because it's his office," explains one father.

"They pay me, I don't pay them," jokes another.

If this sounds like going to extremes, it reveals the kind of attitude—and ego—that makes for success in the relationship. Right from the onset, children should feel that the growth potential in their business is boundless—that they are free to open new divisions, add new products, do whatever they want. That should be the parent's message in the beginning—that ultimately the business is the children's.

"I knew he'd come in," states one father about his son, "and I knew also that first of all, salarywise and otherwise, there would never be a disagreement because I don't care. My family is important to me; whatever they want, they can have. Sooner or later my son is going to be here by himself, or maybe hire somebody else. So while I'm here, I let him do it his way."

So no matter how autonomously you manage business, if your objective for bringing family into the business is eventually to have them take over, be ready to loosen the reins and share the power. Be ready to let them do things their way. A power struggle is a big waste of energy—and a major symptom of failure in family businesses. It's the sort of negative competition that has no positive result. "I love you, Dad," said one son to his difficult father, an autocrat who was unable to relinquish any control, "but I cannot work for you." And out the door he went.

Fortunately, I never had such a situation with Richard, and I don't believe I would ever allow things to reach such a point.

The issue of freedom can be tough, especially when family members are a generation apart and faced with changes. However, as you will see in Chapter 7, there are many strategies families have come up with for handling such conflicts, particularly those that are age-related and involve old habits that die hard. Be careful not to be overly possessive of "what's yours," while at the same time, remember that just because they're family, don't think you can overburden your children with responsibilities you wouldn't foist on others.

Once you do loosen the reins, be prepared to accept the results. For example, if someone you do business with prefers dealing with your child, don't feel insulted or hurt or jealous, but rather feel proud of your child for generating that kind of trust—and proud of yourself for instilling such confidence and for being such an effective teacher.

Question 3: Do I have the flexibility to share high-level decisions about the business?

Incoming family may not know as much as you know about the business, but if they are being groomed to manage it, they should be encouraged to get involved in making important decisions from the first day they arrive.

How do you share decisions?

First, you listen. In any relationship, the ability to listen is a valuable asset; with your children in business, it becomes an essential skill. A son's or daughter's self-esteem is tied into the business on a much more critical level than for any other employee or outside contact, and listening—the first step in sharing the decision-making process—is one of the greatest ways to foster self-esteem.

When a decision is called for, solicit opinions from all family members—and respect those opinions. While Richard and I don't always agree 100 percent on certain issues, we usually give way to the one who makes the best case for how to handle a particular situation or make a final decision.

The difficulty in many businesses is that if the founder made his own way, triumphed over challenges and problems on the way to success, by the time someone approaches him with a new idea he may be so set in his ways that he refuses to listen and insists that his way is the only way.

Now, that's acceptable in certain situations, but it doesn't work well if you're looking for someone to take over, particularly if that someone is family. If you shoot down that person's ideas and make all the important decisions, chances are that very soon he or she may leave and never come back.

Seniority—experience in the business—is sometimes a factor in who gets the final say, but there still should be input all around. In some families, seniority may not even be an issue at all. This was the case with one father who launched a new business with his two grown sons. In their case, everyone grew with the business, and the business grew with them. And because the business didn't start out only as the father's brainchild, the decision making was a true democratic process, with the best ideas winning out.

Don't only share decisions—delegate the authority to let your children make their own. Your offspring are grown-ups—so treat them as such. Show them you are not afraid of potential mistakes—that you trust them regardless of the outcome. (Chapter 5 gives further suggestions on handling mistakes.)

Don't worry about which one of you comes up with an idea that proves successful. If it's good for the business, it doesn't really matter who gets the credit. Richard and I really don't care who makes a particular deal. In fact, we always kid each other by taking credit for things we know the other did. We both believe that who does what is unimportant because it's all for the good of the business.

Looking back on how his father encouraged him to give

his opinion on certain decisions, one son commented, "It's incredibly flattering, surprising—it humanizes business immediately—when you, with no experience, are asked to give commonsense opinions. You suddenly realize that the business is to a large extent common sense—and that you are respected for having it."

Whether in business or not, fostering such self-esteem is one of the gifts parents can give a child and, as one perceptive father found with his three daughters, it pays off in business. "I have an open mind; I listen to them because they are very good," he says. "They are very smart. They know what they want, and they know what they can do. And I have the intelligence to listen to them."

The bottom line is that if your present style of management is to make all the important decisions yourself and you want to bring your family in, now's the time to change. Listen. Solicit opinions. Give your family a feel for decision making, without feeling anxious about the consequences. In time, when you are the one criticized for making a wrong decision—great! It's a sure sign your children have gained confidence in their own judgments, and have the courage to share them.

Question 4: Is my son or daughter really qualified for the job?

Finding the answer to this question requires a truly objective viewpoint because the situation is not always as it appears. Granted, certain personality traits can give clues about one's potential. One parent, the mother of five children, saw that one of her daughters had a special ability to dig in and work hard—she knew right away she was the one best suited to come into her travel agency. And a father saw that because his son had always been "very, very personable; in fact, very funny," he was a good candidate for coming into a business that depended on making people feel comfortable.

While no parent and child can predict exactly how well they will fare together on the job, compatibility only increases the prospects for success. "We have a very similar temperament in terms of the way we look at things," explains one daughter who runs a large marketing firm with her father. Despite her "nonbusiness" background, her father wanted her to come into the company because he saw that certain of her personality traits, as well as her way of thinking, would be valuable assets in the business. Once father and daughter began working together, their thinking proved uncannily similar. "There could be nine, ten people in a room," explains the father, "and I can almost anticipate what she is going to say, and she can almost anticipate what I'm going to say. It's incredible how often we will be thinking the same thing. And part of it is that we have a similar approach to life and certainly to business. It's very bottom line."

As these examples demonstrate, judging whether a son or daughter or other relative is qualified for a particular job involves an assessment of personality traits and compatibility. However, predicting future performance is difficult, and judging it against the past can sometimes be misleading. It does not always follow that a child who has flunked out or largely failed in school will fail in the business. Many a family "ne'er-do-well"—including the poor student who did not finish or even attend college—has turned out to be a natural-born leader in the family business.

Nor does it follow that a parent's positive perceptions of certain qualifications are always accurate. One father did not think twice about hiring his son-in-law, who had done well running a major division of a big corporation. When he came into the family business, he was immediately given total responsibility for finance, even though he knew nothing about the business—and even less about managing money! Having been given full responsibility without any training, the son-in-law—and his relationship with his wife's father—foundered until the need for more background and knowledge was brought out in the open, and a crash course in finance and accounting was implemented.

Any willing child is a good candidate, provided the parent will give the necessary guidance. If working together on a trial basis in the business demonstrates that further education or outside training is necessary, by all means arrange for it. For example, there came a point when Richard and I wonderd whether it would bring more strength to the agency if he went to law school, because we realized that the combination of lawyer/agent might be advantageous for our business and our authors. Ultimately, he did not get a law degree, which was his own decision. He was already well established in the business and felt that in the time it would take to go to law school, he would risk losing the continuity of the business. We figured that we can always seek the advice of a lawyer, when needed.

Question 5: Am I capable of treating my child as an adult?

Are you capable of communicating with a son/daughter as a qualified adult/colleague who is being groomed for leadership?

Families who have successful relationships wisely sort out how they plan to treat their children in a business situation: Should our rapport be formal or informal? Should we behave as partners, friends or as employee to employer? Do we communicate on a first-name basis? Should we use nicknames?

Richard has always called me Dad, and he continued to do so after he joined the agency. Discuss what you want to call each other when you are at work and how you want to present the working relationship to others. Or you, as parent, decide what approach you feel comfortable with and present it to your son or daughter. One father took the latter route because he felt that if he couldn't define the basic work relationship himself, his children were in no position to do so and could easily become confused. In fact, looking back on the working relationship he'd had with his own father, he recalled how awkward it had been. "Many times I did not know where I was with my father," he explains. "Sometimes I was treated as a friend, sometimes as a son and sometimes as the head of the company. I found myself wondering, 'What am I? Who am I?' And since my father could be very, very difficult, until we sorted it all out, I often thought maybe it's not worth it—maybe I should just tell him to go to hell. I'm handling things very differently with my own children—starting with letting them know in clear terms the approach I want to take is a businesslike one."

Regardless of how formally or informally you prefer to interact with each other at work, if you have a good relationship with each other at home, be sure that it is carried over into the business. Don't be a good parent and a friend to your children at home, and then turn out to be a tyrant at the office. The Jekyll and Hyde attitude is sure to fail.

There are a few other attitudes that should definitely be ruled out when parents and children are in business together.

■ The kid in diapers.

If you still see your child as a little kid in diapers, that's your prerogative—at home. In the office, that image must be left behind. Your child is an adult, worthy of all the respect, intelligence and patience you would bestow on any valued professional colleague that you brought in and trained to be your equal. If you find it hard to view your child as a capable adult, do as one parent did and imagine you have stolen your competitor's very best employee—and then treat your child accordingly. Be ready to share the workload so it is spread equally. Be ready to accept the good, the not-so-good and the bad. Don't "protect" your child by hiding the ups and downs of the business.

■ Papa-holding-the-purse-strings.

If your agenda is to have your son or daughter spend three years learning the business because it's "that kind of business," don't pay him or her a flunky's salary. Pay your child as you would any other valued employee and, in fact, if he or she is starting at the bottom, as some experts encourage, consider paying more.

Make promises only when you intend to keep them, especially when it comes to responsibilities and salary.

■ The pal.

Don't intrude into your child's personal matters unless they affect job performance. If that happens, treat your child as you would any other employee you care about, offering to discuss the situation. If they are willing to open up to you, realize that you have a rare opportunity to draw on your own experience at solving personal problems, and that you have a chance to help them sort out dilemmas they might otherwise have carried around for a long time.

Question 6: Do I have the patience and temperament to be a good teacher, one on one? Can I accept mistakes? When I'm wrong, can I admit it?

For many parents/bosses, the most comfortable role seems to be that of teacher. "If you can stand me as your teacher" (Chapter 4 will show you how to do your best), "then come on into the business as my student."

If you can bring an even disposition to such a relationship, that's great. If you have a temper and fly off the handle easily, you will have to learn to keep it in check to be a successful teacher. Nonfamily employees may tolerate your temper, but chances are your family will not, at least not in a work setting; they certainly will not if you lash out at them in front of other employees or business associates. Your apology may be forthcoming, but unless you control your temper, it will inevitably push your child out of the business for good.

"We have our disagreements, but I am the first to give in," one father explains about his relationship with his daughter. "That's because everything I do, including working with her, I do with enthusiasm. Positive and full. I treat her well because I want her to be the best."

While a parent or child's temperament and personality need not be similar, each must make compromises to establish and maintain a successful working relationship.

An even temper is but one aspect of compatibility in the relationship of teacher and student; cultivating a sense of humor is another. Use your sense of humor to dispel tension and to bring a relaxed perspective to your differences. For example, if your son or daughter does not take his or her work as seriously as you do, at least in the beginning, you can let that attitude continue.

Remember, you are not bringing your children in to test them and watch them fail; you are bringing them in to eventually take over the business. Be prepared to:

■ handle them with kid gloves

■ encourage and compliment them

■ accept blame gracefully

■ weigh your criticism carefully

■ take the time to acknowledge and discuss your differences

Question 7: If I can't (mentally or physically) get directly involved in the process of bringing him/her into the business, can I provide a surrogate teacher or middle man who will do the initial training?

You may decide you simply don't have the patience or time to handle the early phase of training incoming family members. Knowing himself very well, one father admits, "I'm probably not the best teacher in the world, okay? I'm a little impatient." This gentleman had the wisdom and good sense to find a mentor—whom he describes as "probably the best thing going"—for his child in a longtime employee who worked with his own father, and who, as the seventy-five-year-old nonfamily president, is not only "very bright and very patient, but also better at teaching than I am."

Providing a middle man in your place is an excellent solution, at least on a temporary basis, as long as you keep in touch about general matters and keep your distance on specific details. You can decide when your child has gained the level of experience at which it would be beneficial to work together directly.

SIX QUESTIONS FOR THE CHILDREN

Question 1: Do I really love the kind of business or the field we're in?

For some, the answer to this question is a clear yes. "This business is like a temple to me," explains one daughter. "I lost my mother when I was very young and this business has always been all-important to my father, whom I idolize—he's a tremendously dynamic person and is considered the patriarch of the industry."

"It's funny," observes another daughter. "You work in a place like this and it's as if I'm in my living room. And I think the people who work here also feel the same in that respect. It's very comfortable here; you're dealing with interesting people and even the problems are interesting."

For other children, reaching an honest answer to this question may require a reexamination of parents' opinions and candidly weighing the pros and cons of working in the business and whether it would be personally rewarding. A trial period on the job may help determine the potential of one's commitment. In any case, the business must appeal to you for you to even try.

One grandfather, who is ninety-two years old and still on the job, describes how he counseled incoming family members about choosing their careers. "When you choose a career," he said, "if it is something that you love, something that interests you, that's already half of the accomplishment. You can take any job to earn money to support a family, but when you do something that you enjoy, especially when it involves working with others in your family, it's so much better for your own success and happiness."

As for a child's obligation to join the family business, children owe no more to their parents than an honest answer as to whether or not the business appeals to them.

Question 2: Do I have a clear view of what the work entails?

If you like the business in general, it is often to your advantage to come in with an open mind about the day-to-day work of the business. When asked if the work had turned out to be what he expected, one son, who couldn't be happier after thirteen years in the family business, said, "I had no preconceived notions about what it would be like; I had no fixed ideas."

In most cases, it's definitely better to be open-minded, particularly if your decision involves working in a field that is gilded with glamour—invariably, such an asset tarnishes fast. After a dose of reality in their mother's travel agency, only the youngest of four children made a career of it. The stress, the long hours, the need for meticulous planning and organization—all of these day-to-day requirements quickly canceled out the appeal of free vacations around the globe. While the other siblings still contribute good ideas to the family business, they now work elsewhere.

True insights into what the work entails are often gained from hindsight, particularly for those who make their decisions in school. Unexpected surprises are not always unpleasant ones either. As one son explains, "If I had known what this business was going to be like before I went to graduate school, that I would enjoy it so much, I probably would have been more determined to come in sooner and might have chosen my coursework differently. When you are a student, no matter what you think the business is going to be like, it never turns out that way. Fortunately, my own uneducated decision turned out to be a great decision because I love the work."

Question 3: Are my reasons for coming into the business valid ones?

When his daughter announced she wanted to come into the family furniture business, one father nearly drove off the road because, as he explained, "she never, never wanted to work as a bookkeeper, and that was the job."

However, the reasons for her surprise decision to come in were, in her estimate, important ones. "I was the only girl in school who majored in electrical engineering, and I was getting a lot of abuse because of it," she explains. "I foresaw that I would always have a male supervisor above me. I looked at that and knew I could never handle it—I didn't want someone always working over me. If I am working hard, at least it should be for me." In the family business, she now has complete freedom handling all the finances and money decisions.

In another situation, a son got halfway through law school before deciding he hated it. Taking time off to decide what to do next, he came in to help his parents on a temporary basis and found out he truly enjoyed working in the family business. Even so, he spent many months grappling with the idea of coming in and overcoming the feeling that he was merely copping out of another career. He soon realized it really didn't matter what he thought. His parents turned over so much responsibility to him that he immediately felt more challenged than ever before.

In yet another situation, a daughter was clear right from the start about why she was coming in. "The main attraction of working here is that even though I know there are going to be a lot of pressures, and a lot of responsibility, I'm here for the same reason that Dad wanted to work for his father: at least I can determine my own future. I much prefer to feel the pressure of that than the pressure of dealing with a boss."

Question 4: Do I have what it takes to work hard—really hard?

How you answer this question is probably more important than defining your initial reasons for coming in.

If you are a workaholic, you are probably well suited for a family business. "I take very little time off from the business," says one daughter who has virtually taken over her father's leadership role. "Seventy-five percent of the year, I work six days a week; ten-to-fifteen percent of the year, I work seven days a week. And then for the remainder, during the summer, I work five days a week. And even then I have to stop myself from coming in on Saturdays to clean off my desk."

Once again, hindsight can reveal the most accurate picture of time commitments. "I knew my parents put in long hours," states one son, "but I never knew I'd work seventy hours a week and not even feel it. I wish there were more time."

Many parents do not expect their children to work as many hours as they themselves put in, but with businesses that run in cycles, no one hesitates to put in double time. The general consensus is that family members do give up a greater part of their personal life or leisure time to their work in the family business than if they worked for another business. "You take your work home with you, and you are on call," explains one daughter.

"We talk to each other every day," concedes another daughter, laughing. "All day, every day, nobody does anything without the others. And when somebody wants something, or needs something, everybody helps. When we have problems, we have a meeting."

However, work does not have to be all-consuming, and many families do set limits as to how much of their personal life they will give up, although some sacrifice is usually inevitable. You've got to decide how much free time and effort you can realistically contribute, and then make it clear to the other family members you are working with.

What are the rewards of working so hard? As one daughter put it—"If you like the industry and are not afraid of hard work, it certainly is very rewarding to be in your own business, together with your parents; having the opportunity to be involved in marketing, pricing, programming, renovations—shaping the business to your own design."

Some perspective on the amount of work you put in is also in order. This same hardworking daughter adds, "When you like what you're doing and you're working hard, what might look very difficult in the first few months, or years, turns out to simply need more time—in the long run, it means less work. Give it time, be patient with it."

Question 5: Do I have what it takes to be a student to my father/mother? To listen to his/her view of the business? To be patient?

One son—now running his father's business—describes a valuable lesson he learned in a family business seminar at Wharton. Incoming family members—children of the founders of various family businesses—were asked to take something they were wearing that they particularly liked and give it to the person sitting next to them. For some people the item was a watch; for others, a ring or other piece of jewelry.

After all the exchanges had been completed, most of the men and women were not exactly sure they liked what was happening.

The teacher then suggested that if the class had a hard time turning over a favorite possession, they should try to imagine how their parent might feel about turning over the business they had owned for twenty-five years. The sooner a child can identify with that, the better off he or she will be in the family business.

When parents bring sons or daughters into a business, they are not bringing them into just any business; they're opening the door onto an important aspect of themselves— a very personal, lifelong investment. The founders of the business deserve respect, and those who come in should focus not on taking over, but, rather, on growing into leadership roles—learning the business and becoming as devoted to it as their parent. That takes patience, a certain humility and time. Children should understand that, particularly if their parents were the entrepreneurs who started the business, no matter what the parents say, nor how much responsibility or what legal status they give their children, as long as the parents are around, they will act as if they own the business. They can sell it, they can give you shares, they can do anything they want, and the sooner you realize that the business is theirs until they leave it, the better off you will be.

In addition, some parents will treat the business as their security blanket. Let them depend on it in that way. They may not have ownership and they may have turned the business over to their children, but they still feel in their heart that it is theirs. Be patient and understanding of how they feel; respect them for what they've put into the business.

Question 6: Do I have what it takes to stand up for what I believe in?

In a healthy working relationship between family members everyone airs his/her views and, as the following "morality tale" illustrates, stands up for him/herself.

A son came to his father and told him he wanted to come into the family business.

The father said, "You can come in on one condition. No matter what I tell you, you will not question me; you will do as I tell you. If you can agree to that, you can come in."

"Fine," the son responded. "I'll do anything you say."

After a few days on the job, the father took his son out to the warehouse, pointed up and said, "See that big shelf up there? Fifteen feet high? I want you to take that ladder that's on the other end of the floor, bring it over here, climb up the ladder, go to top of the shelf and when you get there, I'll tell you what I want you to do."

So the son set up the ladder, climbed on top of the shelf and waited. The father then told his son to go to the other end of the shelf and get the box he would find there. And while his son did as he was told, the father took the ladder and put it away. His son, seeing the ladder gone, then asked what to do.

"Throw down the box," the father commanded. And he threw down the box for his father to catch.

"Now I want you to jump."

"But I'll fall, I'll get hurt," said the son.

And his father said, "But I told you, no questions. You're going to do as I tell you." And after the son landed hard on the ground, hurt and angry, his father told him, "First lesson in the business: Trust your own judgment, look out for yourself."

Whether you are planning to team up together, or are already partners on the job, take a good honest look at how you view your working relationship with family members. Review the relationship often. When asked if he ever questions the merits of bringing his family into his business, one person answered, "Yes, daily." That he's always thinking about it no doubt accounts for his family's successful relationship in the business.

It's been said that a family business is like a big soft lump of clay—if you spend time digging around, pinching and prodding it, you might end up with a work of art. Keep on prodding and poking. Don't tell yourself *maybe* you'll succeed at bringing the next generation into the business; answer each question presented in this chapter with a *yes* and tell yourself you *will* succeed.

3 Planning the Entry Process: Timing and Options

Assuming that a mutual willingness to work together exists between you and your child, this chapter will present some typical options for planning the entry process.

When Richard started working in the office during his summer vacations from college, he kept in touch with me throughout the school year, eager to find out what happened with the deals he had been involved with and to hear about the new deals I was working on.

By the time he graduated from school and began working in the office full-time, he had already had a good dose of on-the-job experience. He was full of enthusiasm for the work, his feet were solidly on the ground and he was off and running in the business.

Would an entry like Richard's suit others his age? That is, dipping their feet in during the summer and then diving in after graduation? For many college graduates, it does indeed represent a viable approach for joining a family business. However, as many family situations demonstrate, there is no one formula. So let me address children who are thinking about going into the family business. Your options include:

■ completing your basic education first

■ seeking outside schooling in the field

■ seeking outside work experience

■ combining some or all of the above

■ forgetting all of the above and diving right in

Despite what you might hear about the requirements for entering a family business—"Get a basic education first!" "Don't come in until you have worked elsewhere, for at least three years!" "Outside courses are a must!"—you are much better off weighing the pros and cons of the options as they apply to your particular situation, and then following your own inclinations. The pros and cons of each will be determined by two factors:

■ *The nature of the business or profession.* Selling real estate or being a travel agent, for example, requires a broader base of knowledge at the entry level (perhaps even licensing) than simple on-the-job training. Of course, professional careers such as medicine or law require no less than three years or more of professional graduate schooling.

■ *The maturity of the individual coming in.* This includes the degree of confidence, scope of experience, relationship with the parent, readiness to learn—in short, the degree to which the child has become his or her own person.

Let us look more closely at the typical approaches mentioned above and see how they might work to your advantage in gaining self-knowledge, and in preparing a well-timed entry into the business.

THE CASE FOR A BASIC EDUCATION

No one is going to recommend bypassing a basic education.

In the words of one father, "An education is something you never lose. When Uncle Sam knocks on your door and tells you what you owe on the money you make from your business, you've got to pay. But what you've got in here," he says, pointing to his head, "your education, that he cannot touch."

The advantages of finishing high school and of going on to college involve many fundamental aspects of growing up—exposure to new ideas that help shape a broad view of the world; making friends among groups of different people; experiencing being on your own, away from parents, at a time when you don't have the full responsibility of making a living.

All of these experiences contribute toward becoming one's own person, regardless of the career you ultimately choose. If the school years help chart the course of coming into the family business, as they did for one young woman who began to think about the possibilities when she was in high school and chose business courses related to the field during her college years, that's a wonderful head start. If they do nothing else but expand your horizons, that too is an invaluable step toward maturity.

But is a basic education, defined as formal schooling, a cut-and-dried requirement for coming into a family business? As we have seen, not always. In some very successful businesses, key family members have no more than a high-school–level education.

Formal schooling can even work against you: If you don't do well in high school or college, it may be hard to convince your family (or yourself) that you are family-business material, when in fact it is definitely worth a try. Remember, many successful business people never even finish college.

Recommendations for Getting a Basic Education

Look to formal schooling more for the world view it can provide than for specific gains in the family business. At the same time, you should not feel compelled during the school years to make the career choice of coming into the family business. If you are not doing well at school or cannot decide on a career, that's okay. If you have an interest in or an aptitude for the business—as Richard's obvious interest in literature helped provide a rationale for our working together—great.

As for completing school, I am all for it. Sometimes just one idea from one professor in one class can influence your whole life. I believe that happened to me when one professor in college told us that no matter what else we learned, we should keep this thought in mind throughout life: *I'm an old man from troubles that never happened.*

I have applied that one sentence throughout my personal and business life and believe me, it works. If you think back at how many times you worry unnecessarily about things that solve themselves by the time the anticipated climax comes along, you quickly realize what a waste of time it is to worry.

THE CASE FOR SCHOOLING IN THE BUSINESS'S FIELD

Specific coursework, and/or preentry on-the-job experience, is an option before *and* after entry; it usually depends on how much of a commitment is involved and how profitable such schooling or experience will ultimately be to the business.

■ Specific Coursework

Many businesses benefit tremendously from an employee's ongoing education. This could include honing up on business management skills and new technology with coursework, lectures, seminars, teaching aids, videotapes or whatever it takes to keep the family on the cutting edge of their particular industry or field. When such courses are available, they offer opportunities for all family members, both incoming and established.

"My father always encourages me to take courses, even now," explains the daughter of a successful residential real-estate developer. "There's still so much that I don't know. And since we are a small company, we've got to be very, very versed in what we do. The market changes so quickly. We could be focused in on one thing today and then find we are into something totally different in the next couple of months. It behooves us to be ready for it."

One mother describes how, when she was just launching her business, "it was the dark ages for women—there were simply no business management courses for women in college." That she can go back for what she missed provides a new opportunity for enhancing her experience and expertise.

In fields that require an incoming family member to have specific licensing or credits, it helps to discuss plans as far in advance as possible among the family members to learn what is involved and when would be the best time to meet the necessary requirements. If the business is cyclical, sometimes on-site experience is a more valuable entry experience than taking time off for necessary schooling.

■ Summer Jobs and Part-time Work in the Business

Many sons and daughters in school who are planning to come into the family business or a parent's profession may consider the option of a summer job or part-time work on the job. In a sense, this is an ideal way to get preentry experience, even if making a career choice to work in the business is premature. In one case, summer work in the family business was merely a good way to keep track of a rebellious teenage daughter. As she tells it, "I was not what you call a model child. So when I was in high school, during summer vacation my parents had me coming in to work with them in the business. They wanted to keep an eye on me. And as a result of doing the little jobs they would give me to keep me occupied, by the time I made a career of it, I had learned the business from the bottom up."

In similar fashion, Richard's summer experiences definitely gave him a jump on early training. As mentioned earlier, part of his training was to listen in on the telephone as I conducted my business negotiations. During one summer vacation, when I was in the midst of negotiating a deal with one publisher, I had Richard listen in on the conversation on another phone. This was a perfect opportunity for him to get an idea of how a top-level negotiation is performed.

I got back on the phone with the publisher, and he made me an offer for the book that, to my mind, was a very good one. However, as an agent, I try to get the most money for a client; I told him I wanted x number of dollars more than he had offered. When he hesitated and began expressing his reservations about going ahead, Richard came running into my office and said, "Dad, put the publisher on hold a moment. I have something to say."

I did what Richard asked, and then he said, "Dad, don't you dare give in to him, because I can tell by his voice— I sense it—that he will pay you what you want."

At that moment, I had to make a decision. Should I listen to Richard's advice and risk losing the deal? Or should I ignore his advice and risk his losing self-esteem and credibility as an equal partner?

I got back on the phone and told the publisher that he would have to pay me what I wanted or I would have to go elsewhere with the manuscript.

He said, "No, don't go elsewhere; I'll give you what you want." At that moment, I had shown Richard that he was going to be important in the business, that his judgment would count for something. And Richard had shown me that he had a talent for sizing up a situation and for negotiating, which is such an integral part of our business.

Part-time work during the school year, if possible, also has advantages.

"I was always working part-time in here," explains a son in a third-generation fine-furniture and woodworking business, "doing maintenance, cleaning the shop, that sort of thing. Because I started at the bottom, I had already built up credibility with the other employees when I officially came in."

He had carefully planned an entry timetable for himself that began during high school when he had the idea of coming into his father's business. He continued to work part-time while in college, at the same time taking business management courses that were specifically related to the expertise he would need in the business, and upon graduation, he came in full-time.

Recommendations for Schooling/ Coursework in the Field

Taking the right courses in school can ultimately prove to be an important part of your preparation for entering a family business. Because of their broad knowledge of what's involved, parents in the business are in a good position to advise their children on which courses would be good to take. By the same token, children should listen to their parents' advice, trusting that sometimes even the most academic-sounding course is worth sticking to when some good can come out of it.

When I was going to high school in the midst of the Depression, I had a cousin who advised me that no matter how tough things got, if I learned shorthand and typing, I could always get a job as a secretary, and even if I never did that, I could put my skills to good use taking notes in college.

I took his advice, even though I was always the only male student in the class. Times remained tough when I finished college, and since I couldn't get a job in the field I had specialized in, I put a "Situations Wanted" ad in the Sunday *Times*, describing myself as a college graduate who was proficient in shorthand and typing. As a result of that one small ad, I must have gotten fifteen job offers at salaries that were about five times more than those offered to many of my fellow classmates. I had my pick of work at a time when jobs were hard to come by, all due to heeding my cousin's advice.

THE CASE FOR GRADUATE SCHOOL

Enrolling in graduate school implies that serious career decisions have been made. In some businesses, an MBA can give incoming family members an advantage, even if it may mean postponing entry or taking time out to go back for the degree. The possible advantages of graduate school may only become evident after an initial trial period on the job. In our situation, as mentioned earlier, Richard considered the merits of going for a law degree but ultimately, and quite rightly, decided against it.

In some cases, such as when family members come in all at once or at least within a few years of each other, an MBA provides added strength at entry level. This was the situation with one father and his two sons when they had to decide which of the sons was best suited to get an MBA and which should focus on the business. After making a group decision, in cases like this, the MBA usually turns out to be a valuable investment.

Graduate school is a given if you are planning to come into a parent's professional practice. Even in such cases, the school experience has been known to upset carefully laid-out plans for bringing children in. One son called his father long distance at the end of four years of graduate school and explained that rather than come into his father's optometry practice, he wanted to stay behind in Chicago and open up his own practice with a fellow student. "But nobody can just come out of school with a fellow graduate and open a practice!" his father responded. "That's impossible!"

"What's the big deal?" the son countered. "You examine a patient, you show him glasses, you sell them to him, you collect the money and that's it. What's to it?"

Hindsight, as always, proved invaluable.

For one reason or another, the idea to open his own business folded and the son joined his father's business as planned. Seven years later, his father began concentrating more and more on what he enjoyed most—examining patients—and he turned over the office work of managing the books, doing the inventory and all the other details to his son.

"And as I took over, I realized that there was a lot more to the business end of our practice," his son concedes. "If I had gone into it in Chicago, opened up a practice with a friend without any experienced person like my dad there, it would have failed. Definitely. Coming in with him turned out to be very smart."

Graduate school can also point children in unexpected directions. The classic stories involve children who go to law school, for example, get halfway through or even graduate, and say, "Why did I ever do this?" All of a sudden, the worthy ideal of fighting for justice gives way to the reality of tax law, wills and estates.

If some careers are killed in graduate school, that's fine. For parents who yearn for their son or daughter to come into the business, but would never push, paying for such time is money well spent—particularly if zero interest in the family business turns into a burst of eagerness to come in.

Recommendations for Graduate School

Unless attending graduate school is necessary to qualify for the business (as in the case of opening a professional office), the decision whether to attend should be made by the child. If he or she wants to do it, fine; it will undoubtedly be a worthwhile investment.

Children should not be pushed into graduate school because parents wish it for them.

Children making such a decision must also consider the time it takes. If one's parent/boss is close to retirement and school would take away from valuable on-the-job training together, it's wise to weigh the pros and cons carefully.

THE CASE FOR OUTSIDE WORK EXPERIENCE

Many parents insist that outside work experience be a basic requirement for incoming family members. While outside work may not be essential for everyone, in light of what it can provide for encouraging individual maturity, there do seem to be some measurable benefits for certain family members. For example:

■ **It teaches the value of money.**

One father with three of his children in the business explains: "It doesn't matter what the job is, just so long as it involves handling money. Children have to learn the value of money—how it's made. Many family businesses fail to teach this important lesson because the parent brings children in, asks them what they want to do and gives them the money to do it. They never find out what it is to make money, because they've always had it easy. Only when they learn the value of money, as their parents did in starting up a business and making it a success, do they learn how to handle and respect it."

■ It teaches the value of hard work.

Working in a starting position elsewhere frees children from feeling demeaned in front of their parents by doing mundane tasks, when very often they won't mind doing them elsewhere. At the same time, it helps build a healthy respect for the simplest tasks in the business and an understanding of why they must be done. The owner of one very successful restaurant in midtown Manhattan, a gentleman who started at a low-level job in the food industry, describes how he still does not hesitate to do mundane tasks. "I check on how it's going, everywhere. If the bathroom toilet is stuck, I'm the first one in there with a plunger. If I see dirt, I'm the first one who cleans up. I look for these things."

■ It helps build self-confidence.

Describing her stint on the outside, one daughter explains that "since I had had the experience of succeeding elsewhere, I felt ready to handle anything. And I felt that I could always get another job if it didn't work out with my family."

"I was promoted very quickly in my previous job," explains another daughter. "I found out I was a hard worker and saw I had capabilities for making business decisions I never knew I had before."

■ It encourages the development of identity and independence—at a distance from family.

"Going out and working a couple of years on my own, I was a whole different person—my own person—when finally I joined up with my mother," says one daughter. "I learned how to make my own way," explains another.

■ It helps pinpoint mutual assets within a family.

In working in an outside job, "more and more I began to see how I could be good for my father's business," explains one daughter, "and how it could help me, as well."

Says one son, of his experience, "I saw how others were working—what they were doing right and wrong, and I think I brought a lot of professionalism to our family business. That's something I don't think my father ever could have done because it gave me my outside view, which is one of the reasons why when I hire people, I tend to hire from big businesses. We're not a big company, but I want to get what they have."

In another case, one son who resisted coming into his parents' jewelry business picked up and drove across country, set on proving himself. "And irony of ironies," he explains, "I ended up selling colored stones on the road. I ended up in the jewelry business in a totally unrelated way. And then when I sat down with my parents, I felt good because I had done this thing on my own, and also because, since theirs had always been a diamond house, I could bring something to the business. I didn't go out to look for a niche that they didn't have, but it just happened that way."

- ## It provides a base for evaluating the commitment to come into the business.

"My son wanted to come in and I wouldn't let him," states one father. "And he went to work on the outside. I think it was very good for him—it's worth something when you go work for a stranger, to see what's going on out there."

Sometimes a bad or boring experience working elsewhere points out the positive aspects of working in the family business.

"I was doing a number of different things," explains one daughter. "I was teaching, writing. And I got a little bored with it. I was too calm, too much at peace. I like to shake myself a little bit, so I decided to come in here and just really work with retail."

"When Jonathan went to work in an office for somebody else," explains one father, "he had it rough. He knocked his head against the wall pretty hard and he went through a rough period. And that was good training. He brought something to us."

- ## It provides skills to deal with difficult behavior and temperaments.

"Getting to see all kinds of management in the food business, watching employees come and go when the fighting got bad, I will always treat my own people fairly and well," explains one restaurateur.

One son credits his outside experience for providing a resource he later used in handling his temperamental father. The lesson came from working with a partner in the music-promotion business. "I would yell and scream at my partner and he would say, 'I'm right here, across the room. You don't have to scream at me. It's not going to get you anywhere.' " When he came into the family business and his father yelled and screamed to argue a point, the son had the wherewithal to respond with a simple and quiet, "You're right." It was a style so unlike what his father expected that it worked.

Recommendations on the Value of Outside Work

Evaluate your situation carefully. If outside work could bring in skills that would make the business more competitive and up-to-date, it is well worth considering. If a child's distance from his or her family helps foster personal growth and confidence, it might be the best route for one to take before joining the family firm.

THE CASE FOR COMING DIRECTLY INTO THE BUSINESS

The pluses may seem overwhelmingly in favor of working outside the family business, but there are also advantages of coming into the business directly from school.

As I mentioned earlier, if my son Richard had expressed a real desire to go to law school, I certainly would not have discouraged him. I might have recommended it to him, but I would not have insisted he go unless he had really wanted to. In the long run, his decision not to go did not in any way turn out to be a disadvantage.

I feel that if the rapport between parents and children is good, many of the pluses listed for outside work—from personal growth to learning the value of money—are just as easily available to children who come right into the business after they've finished their schooling. In addition, there even seem to be a few special advantages to this approach:

■ It can speed up the process of finding one's niche.

This one aspect of working with the family presents a special challenge, which outside experience cannot always ensure. When there are several family members of the same generation (siblings, cousins, etc.) working in the family business, it often takes time in the work setting to get a clear idea of the momentum of the business and where you best fit in.

Assessing his thirteen years in the business, one son describes the time it took to establish his sense of place. "I think probably that the first couple of years I didn't know anything about the jewelry business, and then the next couple of years I think I started to find out that I didn't know anything and so after the fifth or sixth year, I think I really started to learn something. And by then I had really found my own place in it."

■ It provides long-term training with the parent/ boss.

Even if succession won't take place for many years, because the objective of bringing family members into the business is to groom them for leadership, coming in sooner provides everyone with a jump on learning the valuable, day-to-day interactions involved in running the business. Gaining experience at the job takes time—the more time with the manager, the more you learn how to manage.

"I sat with him on everything," describes one incoming

son who came in right after finishing school, "from morning to evening. Every day, on everything. So that as I was able to take over, he always just said, 'Okay, now you start doing this.' He never had any ego problems."

The business itself, whatever it is, is the greatest resource for learning because, while theory can be gained elsewhere, the on-site application is what ultimately determines success or failure.

"You can never stop educating yourself," describes one of four cousins whose whole work experience is in the family business. "You can never stop this learning process because business has become much more sophisticated, and regulations change so fast."

Recommendations for Coming Right into the Business

If an incoming family member has a strong desire to come in immediately after finishing school, he or she shouldn't necessarily be turned away. Some children in their twenties are far more mature and capable than others and should be given a chance. If need be, they can always revise their plans after working a short time in the office, when they feel free to say, "You know, I think it would be a good idea if I got a job with so-and-so [out of the field or in the field] so I can see what other people are doing and what we might learn, and then I'll come back."

Parents lucky enough to have children who are willing and able to take control of the business should leave the choice of how to best prepare for it up to the children. Parents can include their input, but should ultimately let the children decide.

Whatever the route taken into the family business, preparing for it increases one's commitment to make it work. Remember, you are making a long-term investment. Review your entry plans and take the optimum approach for your particular situation. If returning to school or working elsewhere will benefit the business or enhance the chances of having a good working relationship with the family, it should be discussed freely at any point.

Part Two

Hot Spots and Pressure Points:

Common Challenges to Maintaining Good Relationships

4 Making the Most of Basic Training

This chapter covers basic training in detail, giving commonsense guidelines for handling the early training period, which is often viewed as a particularly vulnerable phase in a family business, as parent and child seek to balance their personal and professional relationships.

YOUR SPECIAL TRAINING STYLE

How are you going to make the most of basic training? To begin with, give some thought to the approach you will use during the early phase of working together—that is, *parent as teacher*, where the trainee/student shadows the boss/parent and learns by watching everything closely; or *parent as counselor/adviser*, where the trainee for the most part finds his or her own way on the job (and may even report to someone else at first) and turns to the parent for counsel. The latter is a modified "sink or swim" approach, with the parent acting as the life preserver.

■ Examples of the parent as teacher method in action:

"He just takes me everywhere. He takes me into every meeting, and he doesn't even care whether other people bring their kids. He has partners who will not take their kids around, who just won't. And even if he feels that someone may not appreciate that I'm there, you know, he doesn't care. He just takes me everywhere, exposes me to everything, and I guess I just kind of found my own niche after spending that much time with him."

"My father taught me whatever he knew; indirectly I watched him. My kids are doing the same. And they come up with different ideas as they learn."

"My son learned all he has to know of the profession in school. Now I am acting as his teacher, helping him learn the business side of the profession."

■ Examples of the counselor/adviser method in action:

"First I had my daughters learn the taste of good food by cooking with their mother. Which is very important. And then I threw them in. 'Here, do it,' I said. 'Let's see what you can do with it.' And of course, whenever they needed help, we'd have a conference and talk about it."

"I was in the background, watching. Watching every move. In the jungle, the tiger lets the little babies walk out, and she's in the back, watching. She watches every move they make to see that they don't get into trouble. It's how they learned the business."

"My daughter is really running things. I am her adviser. And that's the way things are."

"My father's got a lot of strengths, but I wouldn't say one of them is sitting down with someone and saying, 'This is how this is done'—you know, being a real teacher. That's not his style. He's great in the respect that he gives me a lot of freedom, he doesn't suffocate me like a lot of fathers might in business. He gives me control, which is good."

"I could always talk to my dad, but I reported to other people, initially. And they reported to my father. I always talked to my dad, and I was always welcomed into his meetings. But I started just by imitating what the other people had done. I just copied it. And then I think what happened with me is that I just kept rising to the occasion."

"I would watch what my father was doing and maybe put in my two cents—with the possible exception of finances—he would never have said 'No, keep out of this.' He would let me try this or do this on my own, and he would say, 'Okay,' or he would say, 'No, that's not okay' and he would tell me why."

Recommendations for Choosing Your Training Style

Determining which of these two approaches to use is mainly up to the parent—the purveyor of experience, encouragement and basic knowledge of the job. Before adopting either approach, think about your own situation. If temperaments allow, teacher-to-student may well be the most effective training partnership. On the other hand, because it presumes setting up a certain distance between you on a day-to-day basis, the adviser approach may help the trainee/offspring gain more confidence on the job than if he or she was right by his or her parent's side. The self-starters fall into this group. "From the start," one such daughter happily describes, "I would never sit there and not know what to do, or how many things to do." She, and others like her, might not be comfortable shadowing a teacher/parent, while those children who prefer close guidance and supervision to get started, would. These are the individuals who want to be told what to do and how to do it, at least at first, and gradually form their own ideas on how to work. Based on what you know about each other, you can begin basic training with either the teacher or the adviser roles dominating, and see how it goes.

OFFICE SPACE

Another important consideration for the initial training period is office space, which can have a significant impact on the entry process, the work relationship and the method of teaching you plan to use.

One father, in advance of his son's coming into the business, went so far as to having office furniture custom-designed on a smaller scale for his son, who was supersensitive about his small stature. He did this with his son's approval, of course; the furniture was ready and waiting for him on his first day on the job and it helped eliminate an area of potential anxiety. Another parent, knowing his son was coming into his professional practice, had the whole office redesigned—doubled in size and modernized during the time the son was in graduate school. Planning the new space together gave them something fun to focus on in anticipation of launching their two-man partnership.

Significant changes in office space are certainly not essential to the success of a working relationship, however, and in many cases, the furniture and office space the new family member uses may be nothing more than an existing desk placed in the space that is available. That's fine if everyone is comfortable about it—and if it fits in with the basic approach you plan to use during the training period. In that respect, office space can help you function effectively as teacher or adviser.

If you plan to teach by example, proximity is essential. This was my plan with Richard. In addition, because my main objective was to make him my equal partner right from the start (an attitude you can assume regardless of training style), I wanted to put him in the center of the action. Thus space considerations were immediately important, and the physical layout of the office was designed to help me implement my approach. The office right next to mine was not occupied at the time, so I had it cleaned up, and when he came in it was the natural place for him to be. We kept the doors open so we could hear what went on in each office—and to this day, we do the same.

You can do what I did—supply an office of comparable size next to yours so that your child is privy to all conversations, meetings and routine interactions—or you might even consider moving a desk, telephone and office supplies for your child into your office so that he or she can observe and learn from the best vantage point possible.

If you plan to be more of an adviser and give autonomy right away in certain areas, some distance from each other may be advantageous. You can use phones or intercoms to keep in touch.

Office location can also help to make clear, to both children and nonfamily colleagues, the respective roles you have assumed. The father who redesigned the office so that his son's work space would be much larger than his wanted it to be evident to everyone coming in that his role was as an adviser and that his son was in charge.

Even if you decide to do nothing, keep in mind that people do not thrive in space that makes them feel uncomfortable, insignificant or unsure of their position. In the following instance, a father's lack of a plan for the office space almost caused his incoming daughter to quit.

"The work was very undefined," the daughter explained. "We were four people working in a place where there were two desks. The gallery director and I didn't even have a place to sit. When one of us wanted to have lunch, the other would have to pack up her papers and move."

In fact, this daughter did leave for several weeks, during which time the father initiated a consolidation move. The prospect of new space and all that it entailed not only brought her back, it also clearly defined her responsibilities.

"All of a sudden, stuff started to happen," she says. "We were working with the architect and running downtown to our new space from our uptown location and back again. I realized my father simply couldn't do it all; he physically couldn't do it. So all of a sudden I had a four-month project of building this gallery. From nothing to do, I jumped into seven days a week starting at seven in the morning."

This woman's father did everything possible to convince

her the future would bring improvements in office space, but it was not until they began happening that she really felt settled in the job.

OFFICE EQUIPMENT

At the same time you are considering work space and location, consider also the status of your office equipment. You are bringing in a member of the next generation, and the early training phase provides a rare opportunity to assess whether office machines, computers, and so forth, are technologically up-to-date. State-of-the-art equipment that an incoming member has no fear of using, which will make the business more efficient, is a worthy investment if you can afford it. It may not be necessary to buy such equipment in advance, although in one case it only took a month for the incoming daughter to realize that her father's bookkeeping system was technologically in the dark ages and that a whole new computer system—one that he had neither the time to research nor the inclination to learn—would be a worthwhile, if not crucial, investment. Once installed, it gave her the opportunity to shape her own bookkeeping system and thus gave her a special base of confidence for assuming the responsibility of handling company finances.

FUNDAMENTALS OF BASIC TRAINING

The underlying goal of every parent's training program is simple: to bring out and enhance the innate capabilities and talents of the incoming member so that he or she is capable of assuming full responsibility and leadership for the business.

In nurturing leadership, whether your prime role is that of teacher or adviser, I believe the best bridge parents can provide from entry to full responsibility is to create an equal partnership—that is, bringing children in at as high a position in the business as possible. They'll need guidance from you at first, of course, but it is this attitude of professional equality, from basic training onward, that ultimately keeps the working relationship between family members at a level that's headed for success.

Here are three priority areas in which parents, while treating their children as professional equals, can help them through basic training:

Defining and Implementing the Work Relationship

By defining the work relationship at the start, you immediately establish a professional, businesslike atmosphere that reduces the need for decision making based on family history or emotions.

If your prime role is teaching by example, say so. You want your child to know right away that his or her role is that of a student, watching and learning.

If you plan to be an adviser, coaching from a distance, explain that too. You want your children to know from the start that you expect them to take the initiative, that they are free to act on their instincts, but that you will be there encouraging them.

There is a public partnership to establish in basic training (covered in Chapter 6) and a private one. With the latter, use these guidelines:

■ **Keep a relaxed, emotional distance on the job.**

Leave the family relationship at home. If it helps, as described earlier, consider using first names rather than Mom or Dad, which can convey distance and a whole different image, particularly when you are among nonfamily members.

"We always joke when people ask us how in the world we work together," explains one daughter, "but really the difference is when we're out of the office enjoying dinner together on a weekend and having a few drinks with friends, he's Dad. Here, in the office, he's not Dad. The tone changes entirely."

■ **Be available for answering questions, no matter how simplistic they seem.**

Welcome questions; solicit and encourage them.

As one daughter describes, "Something that is very important, as far as the dynamics between me and my father are concerned, is that I have never been scared to ask him a question. I never felt there was anything I wanted to ask about that I would be embarrassed about asking. Never, ever did he shuffle me off with 'That's a stupid question.' I can't say my father always talks nicely to me, but one on one, there is mutual respect."

■ **Communicate with each other on everything.**

Let your child open and read all of your business correspondence and vice versa. Share and compare the results of telephone calls with each other so that both of you are equally aware of what's going on.

Keep financial ups and downs out in the open. Share the good and not-so-good news about how things are going. In fact, don't hide anything or keep secrets about the business.

"I try to convey to her in daily conversation what my own experiences have been, and what she may run up against," explains one father. "And little by little she's going to learn it, not by my words, but the words are going to help her understand when she's doing something, that this is going to happen. I think that by conveying some of my experiences to her, it will accelerate how quickly she will learn."

■ Stress the insignificance of mistakes.

When they happen, don't make the newcomer feel his or her world will cave in. Give assurance that it's okay. "Go out," one father told his daughter. "Make mistakes. I'll pay for them." (Chapter 5 is devoted to this subject.)

■ Champion your child's success.

"My father has always been my biggest public relations man," one daughter beams. "He has been so supportive of me and always exuded such pride that I believe him. The positive reinforcement he generates on my behalf enables me to do what I can do."

■ Compliment your child.

Don't hold back from giving a pat on the back. Point out what your children do well, and encourage them to have the confidence to simply be themselves. As a parent and their closest relative, you know their strengths, where they are most comfortable; let them know you know. Sadly, one son realized after his father's death that they had never shared the pleasure of exchanging compliments. "I found out a lot about this after he died," explained the son. "He would tell everyone what a great job I was doing, how terrific it was, how I was really running the company and how fabulously I was doing it—but he never told me. He never said to me, 'This is terrific.' "

All people need to hear that they are appreciated. And every time Richard does something that I think is unusually good, I tell him so—and I mean it. He knows I mean it, and that is what is important.

Don't be afraid to say a good word to your son or daughter in your business, or to your employees, for fear that they may take advantage of you. A little thank you or pat on the back goes a long way toward maintaining an amiable and successful work relationship.

Defining and Delegating Areas of Responsibility

Take the time to write out job responsibilities—your own private "personnel" manual for your successor.

■ Define the big picture first.

Set forth the main purpose, the priorities and the ultimate goal(s) of the business.

"The most important thing my father taught us right at the beginning was that the customer comes first," explains one son. "If there's ever a problem, take care of it. If a client is mad, never yell back."

With these basic guidelines, this son understood right away the rationale for how the business was conducted. The big picture gave him the focus he needed during initial training. Be sure to describe the structure of the company, big or small, map out the divisions and departments and who does what and who reports to whom.

■ Clearly define responsibilities.

Explain to children exactly what they will be doing. By knowing their job area and mastering it, their self-esteem will increase. Being too vague will most likely lead to problems. In the case of the daughter working without her own office space, she clearly would have been much happier if she had been told exactly what her job entailed, and that gallery consolidation—the purchase of a new space—was imminent. To this day, she and her father have different views of why their misunderstanding occurred, but fortunately humor prevails:

"She wanted something that would be instantly successful," the father describes. "That her position and her status and everything would automatically come to her. And would be there. Things don't work that way, as you know. So she was not ready to find out how it's going to happen, and how it would evolve to where she would have an important position as an owner. I wanted her to step back a bit, but she wanted me to define what she had to do."

"I never asked you to do that," the daughter retorts, "and I never expected you to do that. That's your idea and it's one hundred percent wrong."

"Okay, I'll accept that," her father answers without a pause, and laughs. "I'll accept anything."

■ Actively solicit and respect your children's opinions.

Let them know that success in business is to a large extent dependent on common sense, and that you value their ability to think.

In the beginning, if your children seem overly dependent on you for guidance and advice, that's only normal. Don't be impatient. Before you know it, they'll be doing things on their own and even criticize you for making the wrong decisions. When that happens, you'll know you've done a successful job of teaching your children about the business. In our situation, Richard now handles things so well on his own that he comes and tells me when he thinks I'm doing something wrong. Far from feeling hurt when he does so, I am delighted.

■ Give children clear authority over their area of responsibility.

"If my son comes to me for an opinion about a sale, I'll give it," describes an antiques dealer, "but then I'll walk away. If I cut him out and treat him like a clerk, he's going to end up twenty years later as a clerk."

■ Don't rule with an iron hand.

If your children do things only as you want them to, they will eventually become disappointed in you and the business. One father, an optometrist, once became so impatient watching his son use new, state-of-the-art equipment for determining eyeglass prescriptions that he took over in the middle of an exam.

"I picked up my stuff and I just walked out the door," the

son explained. "I didn't say a word but just walked out and kept going. I waited about half an hour to be sure the patient had left, and then I went back and told my father that I might make my mistakes but my license was as good as his. If he wanted to examine a patient his way, fine. But if he wanted me to work with him, he'd have to let me examine the way I want."

Ironically, once he'd mastered it, the son eventually conceded that the older equipment was far more accurate and the new device is now gathering dust, but still he made his point.

■ Be open to the possibility of enjoying something you might at first resist.

Stubbornness can be a common trait, especially in the early stages of working together. This same son who walked out on his father describes how he initially resisted showing eyeglass frames, something his father wanted him to do. "I worked four years for this degree and I was not going to use it to try glasses on patients," he said. In time, he concedes, "it turned out I enjoy it. I hadn't expected that I would, but it just happens to be another part of the practice that's fun."

■ Allow incoming family members to feel the business is really theirs.

Let them know that, within reason, they can do just about anything. The process can be gradual, as one son explains: "I was putting in my two cents and then five cents and putting in my ten cents and getting more involved in the things my father was involved in, and getting more involved in whatever I wanted to be." It was his father's style to "give some string, some areas, but a little at a time"—which is fine as long as the starting end is handed out on the first day on the job.

In our situation, I was more than willing to have Richard participate in every area of business right from the start; it just took patience while our contacts developed the trust and confidence in him that they had in me.

One of our authors, whom I had represented well before Richard came into the business, had such a close working relationship with me that when Richard first came in, he confessed that if I ever left he was not sure he would want Richard to represent him. He felt Richard was too young and inexperienced. Time passed, and after he saw how capable Richard was, he said to me, "Artie, I want you to know that regardless of whether you will be in the agency or not, I will always want Richard to represent me, because he has shown that he really knows what he's doing." This made me very happy because it showed not only that what I had taught Richard about the business had taken hold, but also that he had gained the same respect among our clients that I had for him. This is what I wanted to happen, and today Richard probably takes care of more of our clients than I do.

■ Be your child's role model for honest and ethical behavior.

The day-to-day training of entering into the business should also include a discussion of ethics and honesty, the first order of business in teaching children about work. In this case, teaching is always by example.

"I don't tell them what to do," says one father. "I think you can't tell kids what to do; they're simply too smart. You can only lead by example. And if you are a phony, they don't see any meaning in the conversation. If you lie and cheat, and then you tell your kids, 'Don't lie and cheat,' they will think lying and cheating is just fine because they can see you do it."

"The only way people learn ethics is by example," explains another parent. "Our business is very closely intertwined with ethics because your clients must know that what you're selling them is what you say it is. They're paying us for the truth. 'You've got to be very careful,' I tell my children, 'because if you lie or cloud the truth, in time it will always come back at you.' I sat them down right in the beginning and explained how important it is in this business to tell the truth."

"You can't fool your own kids," observes one daughter. "I don't think either my brother or I would be here if we felt that my father wasn't straightforward and honest."

Defining Work Hours and Time Allocation

In addition to describing the structure of the office and job responsibilities, give your children an overall structure for office time—how it is best used, its scheduling and its influence on the business. Let them know about seasonal factors, if they exist, the ebb and flow of the year as it affects meeting long- and short-term business goals; lead time needed for planning, making payments; making their own time priorities. Suggest how to allocate time for priorities; be very explicit. Out of fifty hours a week, for example, explain that ten or however many hours should be spent on such and such an area of their job, and so forth. Of course this will change with experience, but many incoming family members confirm that time allocations help tremendously.

Richard once said, "I wish someone had told me how I

should spend my time. Really sat down and told me what my short-term goals should be. My father never told me to go make money. By coming into a successful family business, the emphasis was not on my making money. In hindsight, I wasted a lot of time in the beginning advising people who had no talent because I didn't know differently."

When I heard this from Richard, I hadn't realized that he felt I could have given him a better understanding of what was expected of him when he joined our agency. I wanted him to stand on his own two feet and just observe what was going on, and I felt he was intelligent enough to find his own way. When I took him with me to meetings and appointments with publishers, editors, authors and others, he was smart enough to realize that he didn't know enough to offer suggestions or advice at that time. He listened and learned the business as he went along. After about two years, he started to give his opinion and thoughts whenever we had these meetings. In retrospect, perhaps closer guidance from me would have helped Richard use his time more effectively, but judging from where we are now, everything has worked out beautifully without my ever having established any structure regarding office time. However, this may not apply to everyone. How you conduct business comes down to personal style, and in some cases it could be that structuring a timetable would be helpful. It depends on the personalities involved.

The ground rules for arriving and leaving the office each day should be the same for children as they are for the other employees in the office; spelled out from the start and taken seriously (see also Chapter 7).

More often than not, incoming family members who are being groomed for leadership have such a strong commitment to successfully joining the business that eventually they need to be encouraged to come in later, and to take time off. If they are willing to take on more responsibility, they are probably willing to spend more hours at the job.

"I would never leave at five o'clock," says one daughter. "I was all ears, wanting to learn and wanting to be important, be a part of it. Basically, I had a real commitment because innately, whatever I do, I want to do it the best I can do it. I don't know if it's going to be great enough, but I want to give it a try."

"In seven years, I have never taken a day off," explains another daughter. "I am in here Saturdays and Sundays if it has to be. I come in to finish paperwork. It's different because all of a sudden it's not that you have to, it's that you feel obligated. There's no telling yourself you have to get your nails done first and you'll be an hour late for work. That doesn't happen."

"It's funny, because when Dad goes away you are not in here forty-five or fifty hours anymore, you're in here sixty hours because when he gets back, you want everything to be in perfect order."

Let children know they can take time off to see friends, to relax. Help them keep a balance in their lives.

WHEN DO YOU CONSIDER THE TRAINING PERIOD OVER?

While there is no set time limit to a training program, initial training can be considered complete, in the words of one parent, when you feel you are finished with the crawling stage—on your feet, and off and running.

Training takes time, especially training for leadership positions. As children are given more and more responsibility, gradually their degree of commitment changes. Encouraged by parents and given freedom to grow, children become self-motivated; their commitment to the job comes from within. It is the fortunate parents whose children get the business into their system and cannot get it out. This, truly, is the most valuable employee you could ever have by your side to help you in steering the business into the future, to successfully make it grow.

One son observes, "My brother and I subject ourselves to our own pressures, which is how we make this business work." And a daughter assesses her own gradual rise to full leadership of the business. "I didn't realize what a responsibility I had. One day it just hit me. It wasn't anything that was really planned; it just kind of happened. And at every event and every turn, I just rose to the occasion. A lot of it has to do with having my father approve of me, not letting me down. And finally I just got to where I am."

Many children consider their period of training over when they have "found a niche." For some incoming family members, the need for such a search never presents itself; they simply move along a given path, slowly and steadily taking on more and more responsibility toward leadership until one day they find themselves in their own position. However, when children are being groomed for leadership in a business where current leaders have no intention of leaving in the near future, or where brothers or sisters or other relatives are already established in the business, finding their own place in the business can present a special challenge.

One daughter in such a situation found her niche by doing things her father would never do, things that he doesn't have the patience for. "For me," she explains, "it's a labor of love."

"I had to define my role, personally," explains another. "And almost create a role for myself. I was the last one to come in. And I had to create a role that was comfortable and appropriate for me. Because personally, that's how I function the best. You have to love what you're doing, you have to be competent and confident. You do not try to be what you are not. I could not think about running the accounting department because there is no way I would be able to do that. And to think that I could, or to try to, would I think be extra effort and not in a productive direction.

"You have to find out what you like about the inside of the business, and then evolve into someone who's experienced at what you love the best. My father gives us room to develop that way; we can do anything we want."

When your child's confidence, commitment and competence are solidly established, and when your clients and other employees are as comfortable doing business with your child as they are with you, the basic training period can be viewed as successfully completed.

Three fundamental areas of basic training are well worth considering in getting your working relationship off to a good start: defining the relationship, defining responsibilities and allocating time. In each area, parents should take the initiative in establishing guidelines.

In defining the work relationship, two effective methods of training to choose are either parent-as-teacher or parent-as-adviser; the choice depends on individual styles and preferences. Office space can be planned accordingly. Give children a clear picture of their job responsibilities and how to allocate their time. Encourage close communication. Your availability and willingness to offer support and guidance at the beginning will ultimately foster the leadership qualities in your child that the business will depend on for its future success.

5 Dealing with Mistakes and Criticism

Because they relate closely to the decision-making process essential for success, mistakes and criticism are two sensitive issues ranked high on the list of hot spots or pressure points that can crop up in a family business.

Providing the means to handle mistakes and accept criticism are challenges in any office, but added to individual family patterns and the fear of jeopardizing close family ties, they become crucial. With both issues, you've already got a head start if you treat your children as equal work partners, showing them the respect such status deserves. Once you've set the tone of your relationship, you can begin to build skills to help your child deal with criticism and mistakes, tailoring—if necessary, tearing down—existing parental expectations. If you expect too much or come down too hard when mistakes are made, incoming family members will become so afraid of risking parental disapproval that they will begin to avoid making decisions or, when they make a wrong decision, will try to hide it.

The surest way to prevent this from happening is to encourage them to try, even if they may make mistakes. "My son did the wrong thing," says one father, "and it cost me a thousand dollars. But you know why I didn't care? Because he made the decision. It was the wrong decision and I told him so, but I also told him I was glad he made the decision. 'Go ahead and make more decisions,' I told him, and I meant it."

Most decisions, even if they happen to be the wrong ones, rarely affect the continuity of a business one way or another. It is more important to make a decision than to be hesitant and not do anything. A decision that may be wrong will only be a wrong decision once, but if your child is unable to make decisions, it would be a lifelong mistake.

Don't wait until your children make a wrong decision before giving your opinion. Let them know that no matter what they might do wrong, it won't be the end of the world, or of the business. Talk about it right away, in those vulnerable first few weeks of working together when they will most want to please you—when they make their first mistake, it won't be so devastating.

THE PURSUIT OF PERFECTION

Consider the well-stated philosophy of one father who is succeeding admirably at working with his son in the office:

"Everyone wants this thing of perfection, but in the long run the world is not a perfect place. Nor is it supposed to be. You have to have flexibility in a family business. You have to understand that your son or your daughter is not going to know as much as you know, is going to require some guidance and that the guidance has to be given without demeaning them. You have to allow them to accept responsibility and make decisions; you have to be ready to recover after the decisions if there is a disaster. And if there is not a disaster, just a wrong, then you write that off as part of the training. You are making a long-term investment here, in somebody you feel you can trust more than an outsider."

Compare this with another father's advice for avoiding the failure he had in working with his daughter:

"Don't set unrealistic goals and expect your children to meet those goals. Don't be as tough on them as I was on my daughter. Let them grow and mature and learn, and don't demand things from them that you wouldn't demand from any other employee. I demanded more of her because in my mind she was better than they were, because she was my daughter, because she was going to be the best—perfection was not good enough, it had to be better than that. And that was really my problem. I would become angry because she wasn't living up to the impossible expectations I had set for her. I used to walk in and think, 'What did she do wrong today?'—for me it was almost an obsession. 'What can she do right?' I used to ask myself. 'How come she did that wrong?' "

One son, currently grappling with his father's expectations, explains the discomfort they cause him. "He always tries to make me perfect. Whereas another boss will accept things up to a certain point, he never stops looking for mistakes that I make. He not only points them out, he searches for them! He's just doing it to make me better, but it gets really frustrating."

This father would be wise to balance his criticism with a few compliments and accept the following truths:

■ *There is no such thing as perfection.*

■ *There is no way to get more from children by pushing them harder than others on the job.*

■ *There is no one standard against which to judge performance,*

certainly not against yours. Just because you own the business
does not mean you are the only one who knows how to run it.

As one father said, "I have never done anything right in
my life. But I always tried to make it right. I just got in
there and did the best I could. As long as you're doing
something, you're going to do it wrong. It can be improved.
And if you don't get in there and improve it, you're nowhere.
And that's a fact. With all people. And if anyone thinks
they do things right, they're only kidding themselves."

MISTAKES

Let's look at the ways some families are dealing with mistakes, from three vantage points: before mistakes are made;
as they are made; after they are made.

Anticipating Mistakes

Don't.

There are many problems you can worry about in business
that never happen—give them a little time, and they either
solve themselves or people never notice they happened.

Parents tend to worry far more than their children about
making mistakes. Children today have more guts than we
ever did, particularly when they are coming into a business
that has been successful. It may have to do with differences
in their educations, at least in some cases, or it may be that
older people simply have more experience to draw on, and
anticipate problems or mistakes that can occur. One son
observes how his father's caution in telling him to be careful

about avoiding mistakes in the business "is probably similar to what a parent feels when his daughter is seventeen and going out with a guy, and not going to come back until midnight. The father is reluctant to let her have her independence, thinking that she shouldn't be out at all until she knows as much as he knows."

When his father tells him what to do or not do, it's based on his own experience and yet in this case, the father wisely gives his son room to make his own mistakes and experience the consequences. "Only then," he says, "does the reality sink in."

Other parents handle mistakes in a similar way. "Just because you feel like you know the ropes, you can't say 'Do as I say,' " explains one mother. "That's really the wrong attitude to have. Because you really have to give them their own chance to find out right and wrong."

Of course, you don't tell your children to do whatever they please and that you don't care. Giving guidance to help them avoid mistakes is time well spent, as one father realized in hindsight. "I think I should have been a little tighter in supervision in the beginning," he says. "I was a little too loose. What happens is that you always have a lot of faith in them and not that they are wrong, but they just didn't have a lot of learning experience at twenty-four, twenty-five. I thought them to be thirty, thirty-five, and they're really not."

In fact, an awareness of the gap in age and experience can help in approaching mistakes. Parents beyond fifty are in their power years, while their children, coming into the business in their twenties, still have a distance to explore, and grow and mature. The twenties and thirties are learning years and to expect more, as illustrated by the father above, can prove unrealistic.

If incoming family members are free to try out their own

ideas, it follows that they should also be free to make mistakes. Encouraging his daughters to go out and establish their own niche in the family food business, one father said, "Do it. Don't worry about mistakes." He was there in the background, of course, but he knew that if he emphasized the possibility of making mistakes, he would make them nervous and uncomfortable.

You can't be afraid to be criticized. Observing how his son developed a good rapport with the company's most valued clients, one father says, "You can't push in and say, 'No, no. That's too important a client for you.' You cannot undercut somebody's legs all the time and expect him to walk tall the rest of the day. If he louses it up, he louses it up. But that's part of our development course, in any case. And I think the problem that most family businesses face is that they are not willing to tell a big and important client that a mistake happened. It happens! And you have to say it's part of the learning process."

How to Deal with Mistakes as They Are Made

Murphy's Law points out that no matter how slowly and carefully you do things, mistakes will happen:

> *Nothing is as easy as it looks.*
> *Everything takes longer than you expect.*
> *And if anything can go wrong, it will.*
> *At the worst possible moment.*

Don't rush in and tell your children that they are doing something wrong. Be there for them, but give them room to test the waters, to take a swing and miss. Trust them to figure out for themselves how to correct their own mistakes.

In our office, we had a situation where Richard had been working with an author whose latest book was a best seller. Richard gave him an idea for his next book and the author proceeded to write an outline for it. When the outline came in, Richard thought it was great. But when I read it, as I told him, it just was not very clear to me. And I didn't think it would be clear to the publishers we would show it to. I didn't argue with Richard, and he went ahead and submitted the outline to a couple of publishers who normally would have wanted it because of the track record of the author, but instead they all returned it with different suggestions because they too found the proposal unclear.

You must have patience with younger people in the business; let them discover their mistakes for themselves. If I had fought with Richard, he probably would not have conceded that perhaps I was right, but would have continued to submit the proposal and receive unfavorable responses. However, once he'd discovered this through the comments of different editors, he went back and made the changes in the proposal that were necessary. Having the patience to give children an opportunity to make mistakes will, ultimately, allow them to discover that your input is worthwhile. Next time, they'll listen more closely and avoid making such mistakes.

One son, recalling his own mistakes, wisely counsels, "Never look at things and ask yourself what you should have done about this. Instead, ask yourself what can you do right now, right then and there, and also in the future."

This philosophy has worked time and again for him, and he encourages other incoming family members to try it. "It really works in any business, but particularly in a family business," he says, "because if you say, 'I should have done this to make them [parents] happy,' you're lost. It's better to say I could have done that but I didn't do that, so let's go ahead and see what else I can do, move on to the future."

Sometimes it is tempting to fall back on personal connections with a parent. Says one daughter, "When there's a problem or panic, my inclination is to turn to her and say, 'Mom, help me!' instead of staying on a business level with, 'What do you think about the problem?' "

When she hears the call for help, her mother doesn't jump right in. "This is a good lesson for her," she reminds herself. "When she realizes how the error occurred, it probably won't happen again."

There is a theory in management that supports training people by explaining why things are done a certain way, what the logic of the method is and then allowing people to make mistakes. When they make mistakes, you explain why it was a mistake without blaming them for making it.

You've got to let children make decisions and if they make mistakes, don't try to stop them. Instead, tell them, "We'll fix it later." Otherwise, they'll be so nervous about making decisions, it is likely that they will make the wrong one. Let them make mistakes and then sit down and discuss them calmly.

How to Cope with Mistakes After They've Been Made

Encourage your children to come to you right away if a mistake has been made. Don't let them be afraid to tell you about it. Let them know what your attitude is, that if they make a mistake the world is not going to come to an end.

In counseling his sons when they come to him, one father simply says, "Don't do anything. Wait. See what happens," and usually nothing does.

The best message to impart to your children, as soon as

they have made their first mistake, is that life goes on. They'll learn, they'll see what the problem is. Even if you lose time or money, they probably won't make that mistake again, and they won't be afraid to keep making decisions either.

Remember to keep your temper in check. Don't be too tough on your children simply because they are your children. Treat them as you would any other employee. If you were to yell at other employees when they do something wrong, they'd all walk out on you. And, certainly, if you chastise your children in front of other employees, the employees will have no respect for them. "He never let me or anyone else in the office forget my mistakes," describes one son ruefully, who has given up working with his father.

Of course, it is easy when you don't have a temper. Although my son does have a bit of a temper, his anger blows over right away and he'll come back to me a few minutes later saying, "Dad, I didn't mean it that way." He knows he's said something that may have hurt me.

There are parents who, in the midst of confronting a mistake, become angry no matter how hard they try to avoid it. Children who accept this about their parents are at an advantage because they have a head start in developing skills to deal with it. "My father was very much the type that would yell and scream at you," explains one son, "and where others would go back and yell and scream back and defend their position, even if they were wrong, I would look at him and say, 'You're right.'

"And he would be so shocked, he'd say, 'What?'

"And I would say, 'You're right. I can't argue with you. Look at the mess we're in. I can't believe I did it. And I'll never do that again, so now what can we do to make it right?' "

The message here is "Hey, I made a mistake and I'm sorry." Respect it. And then forget it.

CRITICISM AND COMPLIMENTS

Since praise leavens criticism, learning how to give compliments is a prerequisite to learning how to criticize.

Recently I came across an interesting article on the value of giving compliments that supported my own philosophy of treating incoming family members as equal partners in the business. It described how Mark L. Knapp, Ph.D., professor of speech communication at the University of Texas at Austin, in a study of compliments in the work setting, found that 71 percent of all compliments were aimed at colleagues who were viewed as equals on the corporate ladder, 22 percent were aimed at those viewed superior and only 7 percent were addressed to those considered below one's defined status level.

On-the-job equality is thus shown to encourage compliment-giving. Compliments are a necessary part of the cycle to increase outstanding performance. Because of their personal connections to you and their intense desire to please you, your children will thrive on the well-deserved praise you give them.

Notice when they do a good job, pat them on the back when they deserve it. Don't save compliments for later, when the momentum is gone.

"You've got to praise them when you've got to praise them," says one father, "and when they do something wrong, you say, 'Let's straighten it out.' "

For their own well-being, don't avoid criticism, but approach it with sensitivity. Otherwise, as one father who candidly admits "picking on" his daughter found out, they will leave.

Handling Criticism

Neatness, dress standards, punctuality—these are areas in which petty criticism most often occurs. Don't voice your opinion on these matters right away. Observe the extent to which the quirks and habits that may drive you crazy affect your children's performance.

Not too long ago, Richard's office typically looked like an earthquake hit it; I'm neat, but I left him alone—he knows what he's doing; his success proves it. One day when I came into the office, to my great surprise and shock I saw an absolutely clean desk—something that I hadn't seen since the day Richard started working full-time. I used to kid him from time to time that since most of what was buried on that desk had probably been there for the last five years, he could easily just take everything off, open the window and throw it out. He'd laugh and say, "Dad, don't worry, I know exactly where everything is." And he really did. However, to this day I still don't know what made him suddenly decide to clean it all up. But let me tell you, the office looks much bigger, and every night before he goes home, his desktop is clean. I guess it finally became clear to him that people would be much more impressed with a clean desk than with something that looked like a storm hit it. Whatever the reason, it was totally his decision to organize his office. To repeat—if business is going smoothly, don't try to change each other's work habits at all, despite your different styles.

Even with those habits that do affect business, try to change them gradually, not all at once. And when making suggestions, don't sound like a critical teacher, but rather a friend, discussing them calmly and tactfully. Remember, you are not speaking to a child but to an equal partner—you are giving feedback, not harsh criticism.

Children may take certain liberties in a family business that nonfamily members won't. If they feel they need not conform, let them know in a gentle but reasonable way that they must.

"There were times when he was always after me," says one son, adding, "I think ultimately correctly, about the way I would dress when we had people coming into meetings, about making an impression." This son respected his father's viewpoint and it never became an issue. (See also Chapter 7.)

"It's funny," says one daughter about her father, "when he does criticize me he does it in such a way that it's not personal. And it's strange, sometimes I think he's too hard on me and sometimes I think he's too easy on me. I go back and forth. I know he does expect a lot—he does, really— but then he's not a controlling person."

This daughter then went on to make a most important point about accepting criticism: "When you work in a place where your goals are tied to the company's goals, that's what it comes down to. My father really cares about the quality of the work we do. We are very proud of that. And I think people here sense that, and strive for that too. I can really relate to it." Clearly, this woman sees beyond the day-to-day pressures of the work situation, and understands her father's well-intentioned criticism—that it is aimed not at her but at their mutual desire to do their best.

Tips for Parents to Follow When Giving Children Constructive Feedback

■ Make it your business to look for, and comment positively on, things your child is doing well on the job. Too often, competence goes unnoticed, so that all children hear—and tune out—is what you say about their weak spots.

■ Balance negative feedback with positive comments, and ask children to help come up with a plan for correcting a mistake or changing a work pattern.

■ Never unduly criticize children; stick with the action and its consequences. Again, your feedback is based on your own experience. Suggest and examine alternate ways a situation could have been handled that will be constructive, not critical.

And what happens when a parent's performance is criticized? It will happen—it *should* happen, if not right away, then certainly as your work relationship progresses. "She's a lot tougher with me now than she was in the beginning," one father observes. "My daughter is not in awe of me," states another parent. "In fact, she bothers the heck out of me, she tells me all the mistakes I do and she's my critic."

Remember, when children reach the point where they will debate and criticize parents as business partners, that partnership can definitely be viewed as a success.

Let's review some of the points in this chapter:

■ Let your children know that there is life after an error is made. Review the situation with them, but don't get mired in it. Respect—and actively solicit—their opinions. Show them that business is to a large extent common sense, and that you value their ability to think.

■ Don't rule with an iron hand. Try to avoid being nervous about the possibility of mistakes being made.

■ Don't force work on your children they don't feel comfortable doing.

■ Be patient if children seem overly dependent on you for guidance at first. Positive feedback from you on jobs well done will encourage their confidence and independence in making their own decisions.

■ Refer to the business as "ours," not "mine," right from the start.

■ Don't say anything to make your children feel beholden to you when they become a big success, such as "Where would you be if it weren't for my bringing you in here?" Such a statement echoes back as one of the most insidious criticisms a parent can inflict on a child.

■ Let your children take all the credit for being a success in the family business; they certainly deserve it.

6 Working with Nonfamily Members

The work relationship between family members does not exist in a vacuum. It affects, and is affected by, the colleagues, coworkers and outside contacts on which the business depends. Parents can take the lead in keeping work relationships harmonious. They can prepare nonfamily employees and children for the prospect of working together and provide skills for establishing a mutually beneficial, on-the-job relationship that will remain strong after they have left the business. This chapter provides ten basic suggestions for working with those in the business, followed by suggestions for working with outside contacts.

WORKING WITH NONFAMILY, INSIDE THE FIRM

- **Prepare your staff for your child's arrival.**

Don't be vague. Once you have decided to bring your child or any other relative into the business, provide ample time for others to get used to the idea that the next generation of family is coming in. Let them know that while business will continue as usual, a family member will eventually take over. You need not make speeches or send official memos, but in a low-key manner make it clear to everyone in your organization that your child will gradually become an important member of the business.

To help employees who might feel threatened by incoming family, be very specific about what your child will be doing, and to whom your child will be reporting. Tell them about the equal partnership you are establishing; it can help diffuse potential insecurity because it implies that nobody is going to be displaced or lose his or her job.

Of course, there are always exceptions, as when the business takes an unexpected turn and you do what is most expedient for the future. In one foundering marketing firm, when the father fired most of the existing staff and unexpectedly brought his daughter in to try to navigate the company back on course, there were hard feelings to deal with. Explains the daughter, "There weren't that many people left, but there was one woman who thought that whatever position I had, she should have. She had already put in the time, she knew the business, I didn't know the business—she felt I had the job because I was the boss's daughter, and that she deserved it. And it took a long time to bring her around, but the whole situation was nothing that any of us anticipated." Obviously, you do what's best for the company and, if it should arise, weather nonfamily resentment.

■ Prepare your child for working with staff.

It is often more difficult for members of the family to be accepted by coworkers when they join the family business than it is for a nonfamily member. Incoming family members are thrown immediately into the spotlight, closely watched and, possibly, quietly or openly criticized. Give your children ample time to get used to the idea of working with your other employees. Let them know you are proud of the people who work for you, that they are people who share your own goals for the company's success. (Hopefully this is the case; if not, you should attempt to clarify such goals with them.)

Candidly explain to incoming family the personality quirks and attitudes of the key players in your business as you perceive them. Offer ways to help them win over these key players. In particular, stress that there is much to learn from those on the job, if they are receptive and attentive to the possibilities. "All of what I learned comes from working with all the people here," one daughter freely admits.

In some cases, particularly when there are disputes between family and nonfamily employees, parents must let their children try to work things out for themselves. As one father explains it, "The supervisor where my daughter is working is very talented technically and very bright and works well with customers, but in some ways he resents her involvement in supervision. He plays games where he tries to maneuver me around my daughter and it's very complicated because he's an important person in the company. But people do that. It's very difficult for my daughter, but it is something that she will have to learn for herself, how to work with these people. I discuss it with her, I advise her, but I can't completely help her because I have to run the business. And everybody knows that she's going to be running the business when I leave, I always tell them that, so somehow, she'll have to find the way to work with them." With the situation being dealt with out in the open, undoubtedly this daughter will find her own way.

■ Show your children the value of using tact and diplomacy with coworkers.

Teach them how to use tact and diplomacy effectively to win over key employees who have worked long and hard in the business. These people need to be appreciated too, especially by the boss's would-be successor. Being receptive, and respectful of their knowledge and expertise, can take you far in this respect. "If you want to learn, you can learn a good deal, but it all depends on how you go about it," explains one father who worked at his family's newspaper. "Everybody who worked for me was twenty years older than I was, but I knew if I said, 'Me captain, you sergeant, this is how you'll do it'—it would never work.

"Instead, I would sit down with them, explain what I wanted to do, and then say, 'You're experienced; how do we go about accomplishing this?' Or, 'Do you really think we need to do this thing this way? What about that way, which may save us more time?' Going about it that way, their response would always be a positive one—'I hadn't thought of it that way; that's a great idea.' "

While such an approach comes naturally to some children, for others it takes a parent's guidance. "My son used to come in and expect the men who are working here to listen to him," explains one father. "And I said, 'You can't do that. You can't take a guy who's working here fifteen, twenty years and all of a sudden you walk in off the street and expect him to treat you like the boss. You've got to earn that respect. You've got to show him that you're willing to work with him, and learn from him, and that you understand the work."

When some of his employees jibed his son about being family, this same father wisely counseled his son that he would be sinking to their level if he defended himself by arguing. He advised his son to ignore their comments and let his actions demonstrate that he could work as hard and as competently as they did.

■ Remind your children that they will have to earn the respect of nonfamily members.

This applies to both employees and outside connections.

If there is any advantage in starting "at the bottom," it is having the opportunity to gain the respect of others in the company. "[My brother] didn't start out in the office, he started out on the loading dock," explained his sister. "He's had every job in this factory, basically. He went from loading dock to maintenance man; he's had the grimiest jobs in the place. And the employees, they know that. They'll see him in his coveralls, covered in soot from head to toe, walking around the place. It's not like he's a prima donna. He does a lot of lower jobs than they have to do."

Of himself, he says, "No one in the shop can tell me I don't know what I'm doing because I have learned it all and done it, and they know it."

You don't have to start at the bottom to be respected. At any level, respect is earned. "He's not just the son of the boss," said one employee of an incoming son who came in to handle sales orders at a very busy time. "He did a good job and followed through." Do your job well, and the respect will come from those who watch and work with you.

■ Use the opportunity of bringing in family to review your rapport with staff.

As always, insights into nonfamily interactions from those who have failed at bringing in children can be valuable.

"Would I do it differently?" questions one such parent. "I

am doing it differently. I treat my other employees better than I did before my daughter left. I delegate work. I delegate authority. I let them do it. I never used to have a staff meeting—it was always, do this, period. Today I have staff meetings with my key people. It's a whole different feeling that I have running my business, and I attribute that to the experience of learning the mistakes I made in losing my daughter."

Treat high-level nonfamily managers with kid gloves during the early training period. Introduce them to your children by crediting them with their successes in the business. Look for ways to compliment them as often and as publicly as you compliment your offspring. "It's a question of values, approach," explains one of four third-generation owners of the family business, "of encouraging other people to participate in our growth. The way I run my department is to give credit. Let them know they are part of the decision-making process, and let them enjoy that credit."

In another situation, family members make an all-out effort to involve nonfamily members. "We talk about the major issues. We have a planning committee in which people in our company other than members of the family participate. We try to operate by consensus, rather than by edict. Because this is a creative business, we want our people to work in an apolitical situation; when the spark is there, develop it. Solve our customers' needs. Family business or not, we never lose sight of the fact that ultimately it is the customer we have to satisfy, not ourselves."

■ Be fair to other employees.

Treat nonfamily employees with the same commitment and neutrality you would your own family members.

Be ready to promote from within, to hire competent

nonfamily employees for management positions. Don't think that you or your children are the only people who have enough skill or talent to run the business. Bringing in outsiders with particular skills can add to the overall value of the family business.

Ideally, you want to make everyone in the firm feel like a member of the family. In a world where trust is a rare commodity, nonfamily employees who feel they can trust you are going to be that much more loyal.

"We have a strong sense of responsibility to our employees," says one brother. "We don't have five families to feed, there are one hundred and thirty families. If things are bad, they come first. We come second. The most important thing is the health of the company; our employees. We'll worry about ourselves after that."

■ **Show your children that you support and, if necessary, defend nonfamily employees.**

"One day a patient called up and was giving my secretary a hard time," says one father, "and of course she's so very conscientious that she was in tears. And I said, 'Let me talk,' and I took the phone. 'You're very unfair,' I said in a matter-of-fact way to the caller. 'My secretary explained everything to you nicely and you've got her in tears. Now you talk to me.' "

■ **Set a good, professional example among all the employees in the firm—with an emphasis on the nonfamily, company structure.**

Sometimes, the working atmosphere of a family business can, as one mother describes, be "good and bad—you become so family-oriented and extend yourself in such a way that other employees can't help but take advantage of it. Sometimes," she continues, referring to herself and her daughter, "we just have to remind ourselves that we are the bosses."

One way to emphasize the nonfamily business structure is to keep the office talk between family *about* family down to a minimum.

While it is impossible for a parent and a child not to discuss family matters in the office from time to time, make sure it does not interfere with business. And under no circumstances should you inadvertently let your employees suspect you are discussing "business secrets" that might involve them. To avoid suspicion from employees who might see the two of you chatting confidentially, keep your office door open. If it is a very personal matter, don't talk about it in the office at all. Take time out to have lunch together to discuss it.

■ **Anticipate the effect of growth on interactions with nonfamily employees.**

"As you become more of a boss and business grows, one of the things that happens is that people don't always tell you what's wrong," explains one very successful brother in business with another brother and two cousins. "The most important asset we have is our employees. We want to be visible; we don't want to be locked up in an ivory tower and distance ourselves just because we've grown. We touch the people who work here. They know that family people are here and that we want them to succeed."

He goes on to explain that "as the business became more successful, our goal was to defamilyize the running of the company, so that instead of being strictly a family structure, it should be more like a corporate structure—but with a family feeling. That way, you lose some of the emotions that come into play in family business, and it also gives you a chance to establish middle management. In a lot of families, the people who helped develop the company don't want to let go. They don't want to share the leadership roles. So what we've done is establish a title that means something. If the person is a manager, they manage. If they don't manage, they shouldn't be a manager."

■ **Don't allow family members to "squeal" on others in the organization.**

If they are viewed as your "spy," your children will never be trusted. In this situation, an equal partnership between the boss and child is advantageous because your son or daughter has as much authority to resolve problems as you have. You might discuss procedures together at first, but when your children work one-to-one, let them handle whatever problems they discover among coworkers. "When I first started here," describes one daughter, "there were people used to getting away with so much, long before I came in. I started from behind, and when I came up forward, they couldn't pull things because I had as much experience as they did and knew what was going on. They knew I was really the boss, and yet it still took a while, including turnover of staff, before my position was fully understood."

WORKING WITH OUTSIDERS: CUSTOMERS, CLIENTS AND CONTACTS

The speed with which outside contacts build rapport with your children depends in large part on the nature of the business—the pace, the level of stress generated, the general atmosphere, the amount of trust and interdependence that is required to do business. In fact, the high-stress situation can be to your advantage because there's very little time for outsiders to make judgments about working with a "family."

■ Inform your children who the key outsiders are to your business, and impress on them the value of these outside contacts to your success.

Don't hold back on your own personal impressions of certain individuals, but stress that the manner in which your children approach all outsiders should be one of polite respect. Teach them to be gracious and pleasant in all their contacts with clients or customers; the customer, even the most difficult one, is always right—up to a point. Be realistic too. Eventually, you can decide between the two of you who is better at handling certain people, and then do business with them accordingly.

In my own case, from time to time, there are certain editors or even authors who, for one reason or another, can just rub me the wrong way. Although we have great confidence in the work we do and the representation that we give our authors, we cannot satisfy everyone at all times. So if there is a conflict of personality or a lack of understanding, I will say to Richard, "What do you think of your talking to so-and-so from now on because every time I do, I feel my blood pressure going up." There are times Richard feels the same way; both of us are ready to interchange our responsibilities. Personality cannot always click, and those are the times when it is wise to discuss it and decide who will take over.

■ To establish your children's credibility with outsiders, do not define your business in terms of family—but in terms of talent and aptitude.

Let the outside world know the business exists and thrives because of the talent within it. Indeed, the rapport incoming family members have with insiders and outsiders alike ultimately depends on the performance, effort and honesty of everyone involved. If your children are doing a good job, that will become evident soon enough. "If you spend time with my daughter," explains one father, "then you know you are dealing with a substantial person. That's a very important factor in almost any business, but in the art field it is especially significant because that's what you have to sell—your knowledge, your integrity and your taste. If customers have no confidence in your taste, if they have no confidence in your integrity, you're not going to sell something to someone for two million dollars, whatever it is."

You can convey the confidence you have in your children's abilities when you introduce them to outside contacts and clients, but then you must give them room to demonstrate that they've earned it. This was my approach when Richard came into the business, and it has fulfilled all my expectations and more in winning over our most valuable clients.

■ Decide how you will address each other in public.

It doesn't hurt to be somewhat formal together when you are with outsiders. Remember, if you have a good relationship at home, there is no reason to become a different person at work.

■ Introduce your children to key outsiders
yourself, with great pride.

Let your most valued contacts know in a businesslike manner
what your son or daughter will be responsible for at work
from now on, and refer to your child in a manner you would
use if you'd hired away a competitor's most valued employee.
In fact, your child is even more valuable because he or she
may be the very person you have been waiting for to entrust
with the eventual leadership of your business.

■ Stress that your children's authority is equal to
yours.

An equal partnership works to your advantage with outsiders, possibly more than with insiders, because of the
status it suggests. The process of building trust in the competence of your children may take time, but if outsiders are
shown that they are being groomed to eventually take over,
they will be ready for it all that much sooner. Clients want
to deal directly with the decision makers in the business,
not with assistants. If you present your children as your
equal, their position will, in time, be held in as much respect
as yours.

■ Prepare your children for the possibility that
outsiders may prefer to do business with you.

Even though it may never become an issue, your child
shouldn't feel hurt or insulted if it does. If some clients/
customers want only to deal with you, because of the personal relationship you have developed over the years or
some other factor, respect their desires. Chances are, as
with the situation with Richard described on page 99, it

won't make any difference after a while which of you they deal with. A much more likely situation is that new clients may only want to deal with your son or daughter, particularly if those clients are the same age as your child. In creative or innovative fields where young people dominate, age seniority usually has little effect on how business is done. "In this field, there aren't a lot of family businesses, but there are a lot of people my age who are directors of galleries," one daughter elaborates. "You don't see someone my age running a manufacturing company."

Of course, many times close relationships are of no consequence at all in doing business and the issue of preference never comes up. "Our suppliers, advertisers and so forth don't even know I exist," explains one father. "My daughter talks to them, and then she talks to me and we decide together on certain things, and they get done." Clearly, this daughter exudes confidence in handling outsiders.

However, convincing outsiders of one's worth can be a special challenge for daughters (and their boss/mothers) in fields long dominated by men. "I find it comical," describes a daughter in one such situation. "All of us in the office, including my father, don't have a quarter of the knowledge that my mom has about this business. Sometimes in the middle of making a deal, the negotiators will turn to look at my father or any other male present and expect him to have the authority when really, nothing gets done without my mother's approval. It doesn't bother me, really, because women are getting more respect in the field, and it doesn't hold us back from what we're doing."

■ Be generous with your contacts.

After bringing children in, many parents notice for the first time that a new generation has come into the field, and that slowly, in certain areas, they can step aside. Many parents are delighted to do so, although parents should avoid feeling jealous or possessive of your contacts or expertise. One father describes how his son gravitated to the customers; having never been particularly good at it himself, he was only too happy to relinquish that responsibility. Another father enjoys watching the widening circle of contacts his son is making, but jokes about how he only gets to see the older customers and how the minute "a woman with a nice figure appears," his son is right there.

■ Praise your children in front of employees or outside contacts.

The more you do this, the more it confirms your own perception of your children's competence and abilities. This not only gives your children confidence in themselves, it boosts the confidence of outsiders as well.

■ When working or negotiating with outsiders, use your equal partnership as leverage in deadlock situations.

One of the advantages of presenting your child as an equal partner to the outside world is that each of you can intervene on the other's behalf or diffuse tension during difficult negotiations. Decide together what the bottom line of your terms will be, and then be ready to come in and negotiate using your own style, but speaking always on the other's behalf.

By example and by initiative, parents can lead the way in establishing a solid, professional rapport between family, nonfamily employees and outside contacts. Communicate with staff and outsiders. Let them know at all times how much you value their connection with the business, particularly when children are first coming into the business, and up to the time you plan succession.

Teach your children how to win the trust and respect of nonfamily employees and clients. Explain how these two basic building blocks of a good, working relationship will take time, that trust and respect are earned.

7 Handling Personal Differences and Age-Related Conflicts

This chapter focuses on areas of potential conflict between parents and family members that may crop up because of differences in business style or age. More often than not, the two are related.

When the primary intent in a family business is to groom the next generation for leadership, early participation in key management decisions is necessary. Family members who work together are often many years apart in age, which accounts for fundamental differences in work style, personal goals, goals for the business and general outlook on life. You can effectively leave all the "family baggage" at home—personal conflicts in your family interactions—and still run into the age-related conflicts that affect both family and nonfamily businesses alike. If not handled carefully, these stage-of-life differences may even pit one generation against the other in realizing common objectives and dreams for the business. With their children in the next office, parents often recognize for the first time that theirs is the passing generation—and they are not always ready for the revelation. Similarly, with their parents in the next office and the path laid out for succession, children may get a sudden urge to pull away and strike out on their own. Of course, when family members disagree, everyone in the office suffers—

nonfamily staff often take sides; the quarreling interferes with communication and disrupts the flow of work.

The following examples are some typical areas where age-related conflicts can arise:

■ *Defining the status quo.* For some parents, the status quo may be defined as keeping the business where it is; for children, it may mean working to streamline procedures and make changes they feel are overdue.

■ *Handling money.* Whatever the area of transaction—negotiating deals, pricing goods and services or paying salaries—when members of one generation put a different value on the dollar than the other, conflicts are likely to arise. In addition, many parents want to hold on to capital, while their children want to use it for new ventures.

■ *Running day-to-day operations.* A parent's way of doing business may run counter to what his or her children want. For example, a child's desire to bring in new equipment, hire new employees or introduce new working procedures can often cause conflicts.

HOW TO APPROACH AGE-RELATED CONFLICTS

Before we examine how families handle these and other age-related differences, let's consider two underlying premises that frequently account for success.

Recognize and accept that an age difference exists.

Once you are aware of an age gap, it can work to your advantage. "Because of his age," observes one daughter about her father, "he takes time during the day to just sit and think. I don't know how to be in here, and think. I don't know how to do that. I don't know how to cut and draw the line between thinking about what I'm doing, and doing what has to get done in the immediate future. That's so important in any business and I think because of his age, he's much better at that than I am."

And one son points out, "Because there's a much larger age difference between the two of us than between most fathers and sons, there's probably a larger difference between our opinions on things." In their case, his father's sense of humor at work breaks up the tension that occasionally develops between them. Concedes his son, "My father establishes the atmosphere in the office. The secretary has a great sense of humor, the optician has a great sense of humor; everybody is trusted, nobody complains. It's a nice place to be." Jokingly, his father comments, "As long as I give him everything he wants, what's to fight about?" He adds a key point: "No, he has a lot of freedom, more freedom than I ever anticipated I'd give him."

Forgetting about the difference in age can easily happen when family members work as equals, but conflicts can still arise when clients or customers don't recognize your equality. As my son Richard explains, "The ten-year jump on a career, in my particular case, gave me access to a very high echelon in the business very early on. The reason was because my father was so well liked, he would introduce me to these important people he did business with, and I would think nothing of calling up the publisher of Simon and Schuster or Putnam or Random House and asking them to let me try selling them a book—when I was twenty-two. Others my age were assistants to assistants to secretaries. As a result, until my late twenties, I had a tough time with being as successful as I thought I should be. I was comparing myself to the most successful people in the industry, wondering why, while I worked like a dog, I wasn't making million-dollar deals every day. And then finally one day I realized that things don't happen all at once—that life is a progression and that the people I was torturing myself about were different from the people I would be working with when I was their age."

Richard realized that some people in powerful positions will just not accept people twenty years younger as their equal. He further realized that "there is a much, much bigger difference between a twenty-two-year-old and a thirty-two-year-old than there is between a thirty-two-year-old and a fifty-two-, or sixty-two-, or even seventy-two-year-old, for that matter." The twenties are really a time for exploration. "Because whether you like it or not," comments Richard, "unless you are an exceptional person, you are still a kid. And that is the time when you shouldn't necessarily try to be number one in your field because you're not going to relate to the power generation, and they're not going to be relating to you. People don't like to do business with kids if they don't have to. And I said to myself, 'Hey, great! When I'm their age, everyone else who is running the business is going to be my age.' "

Clearly there is much to gain by not rushing things and, instead, using the early years in your business to learn about its interior workings and about the industry. As for the following years, in today's business world it seems young people assume power positions much earlier than they did when I first started in business—there's not that long a time to wait.

Admit that conflicts exist.

Families who make the mistake of trying to hide or deny their conflicts always run into problems. It's the ones who grapple with them that survive.

"I've been joking lately about my two sons," reports a father. "When people ask me how they get along, I say they get along great. They have one purpose in common: to get me."

"We fight all day long," states a daughter about working with her father. "We bicker all day long." In their situation, such a style of communication works to their advantage— the back-and-forth debates resemble the kind of negotiations that are essential in their business and require a skill the daughter knows she will need to become more adept at handling business deals.

"Well, this business is built on that, right?" her father elaborates. "You say ten, they say eight. It's automatic. The guy who is bargaining with you is your customer. The guy who doesn't bargain, and doesn't buy, he's nowhere. I couldn't care less about him. It's the guy who says, 'You want six thousand? I'll give you three!'—that may be ridiculous, but I'm not angry. He's a possible customer. We'll arrive at something."

Bringing problems and conflicts out in the open in any business is the first step toward solving them, but in this respect, families in business seem to have a special advantage. As one son explains, "You feel freer in a family business to debate, which has its good and bad points. The freedom is probably what causes most of the arguing in the first place, because if it were someone other than your father or mother, you wouldn't debate as much, but at the same time, you have more freedom to give your opinions and views and have them count, even if they are contrary."

Open debates seem to be a common trait among many families who are succeeding at working together. "Oh, sure, we have very, very open discussions," states one daughter. "And I think some people would be really surprised by it. Sometimes, we will have an argument in front of another officer, right here in the company, a disagreement, and I think it is a surprise to the other person that I would be so free to tell my father exactly what's on my mind or if I don't agree with him."

Debating is usually good because both parent and child can discuss anything that may be bothering them. As one boss/father states, "We vent everything out in the open and that's it, we solve it." And when the debate comes to an end, it should really be over, with no lingering hard feelings. "We don't have time to fester and stew about a lot of this," explains another boss, this time a mother. "We try to move on to the next thing and make it work."

That's really the key—having the so-called debate, trying to resolve the issues and then letting them go. In a family business, this can get "a little sticky" in the words of one father. "I mean, there are times when it's difficult for me to distinguish between my daughter as my daughter, and my daughter as my associate," he says. "But the strength of our relationship outside the office—which suggests the business

relationship is working—is that we don't hold onto problems. This is a pressure business and we don't always agree—
at times she's gotten very irritated at me just as I have gotten
irritated at her—but you cannot avoid this happening in
pressure situations. We don't believe in holding anything
back. If it happens we discuss it, and yet we also don't
believe in harboring grudges or problems."

Recognizing that conflicts do exist, and that each family
member has a different way of resolving them, let's look at
six common areas where age-related tensions can crop up
and explore how families cope with them.

CHANGE AND GROWTH OF THE BUSINESS

"My kids, they want to grow," explains one father. "They
want to make this into a gigantic business, put it on the
market, make it public. Who needs it?"

"They want to expand, and to expand costs money,"
explains another father. "I'm afraid. Because at this stage of
my life, I don't want to gamble. And that's what it is, because
if it doesn't go, you've lost the money. I don't have that
much in reserve."

"You have this office," demands yet another father whose
son wants a bigger, second practice. "What more do you
want?"

When children are brought into leadership roles, it is
foolish to think that the business will remain exactly the
same. Sooner or later, they will push to proceed forward in

a direction that may be quite different, even contrary to what parents intended. While it is a child's right to propose new ideas, the parent obviously does not want to be tagged as an obstacle to profitable change and growth, nor, at the same time, be compelled to add more work hours or lose all their assets.

Issues centering on changes and growth in the business include everything from office space, new equipment and reorganization of staff to changes in the scope of the product and direction of the business—the latter involving outside clients, customers or territory.

Tips from Parents for Handling Change and Growth

■ <u>Make it clear to your children what your limits are.</u>

"As long as I stay here," explains one father, "I want to make sure that if business isn't too good I don't have to fold up. I went through a lot of recessions, I went through a lot of problems and if I hadn't paid for this building, I would have been out of business. We owe nothing, and if we have to shrink down a bit, we'll survive." That's the bottom line for him.

Children coming into the business should understand from the start their parents' theory or outlook on certain matters involving the growth of the business, expansion into new areas and so forth. If parents make their expectations for the business clear in the beginning, their children will not feel hurt or surprised when their recommendations are not accepted later on.

With our business, I did not want to expand to a point

where it would have control of my life, and I would have to worry about slow times, having to fire people and so forth. I always wanted the business to be such that I could have time with my family, go on vacations and do what I wanted. In other words, I would control my business; my business would not control me. To my mind, the difference in profits between limiting the size of our business and letting it expand unreasonably would not be that great.

However, when I am no longer in the business, Richard will make his own decision to expand or maintain the business.

■ **Keep an open mind when changes are proposed, but be ready to put your foot down too.**

"I have to hold them back!" exclaims one father, commenting on his daughters' ambitious plans. "They want to go ahead, but sometimes you can move too quickly. That could also destroy you. It's like the army. With expansion too fast and supplies not coming up fast enough, what do you do then? If you're in a war, and you've got nothing to shoot with? You've got to match demand with supply."

As a parent/boss, you should provide a larger context in which your children can see all the pros and cons of their plans for growth and expansion.

"You see yourself as you get older being much more conservative," describes one father. "I have tried to expose my son to other people and other ideas, and I think that when he sees the whole world is more conservative about what is going to happen in the next couple of years, some of his ideas are going to have to be put on the shelf for the time being."

■ Observe your children and be ready to let them go ahead when their ideas are sound, and when they show responsibility, commitment and competence.

"My son is very capable," states one father. "If he weren't, I'd have to clamp down and maybe say, 'I don't like what you're doing,' and then he would surely be insulted and hurt. Fortunately, he's good at what he does."

In one highly successful New York art gallery where the challenge, as in all galleries, is agreeing on what art to show, the father and daughter concede that because there is a fifty-year difference in their ages, the challenge becomes even greater. The father concedes that in choosing art, "because compromises are not good for the business, she has complete authority to do whatever she wants to do. She will come and discuss it with me, but in the end she makes the final decision. And only if I think she is making a horrible mistake would I bring it to her attention."

■ Be ready to ask your children for their insights, especially when changes in the market require changes in the business.

In one family where several members of the younger generation came in almost at once, one of the brothers explains how "we saw that certain aspects of this business were maturing, and we had to change the structure of the company. We had to look for more opportunities, more products. We were fortunate because the decision to expand the base of our operation also dovetailed with some of the trends that were going on at that time."

In this family, the younger generation was able to make

changes and increase the success of the business in ways their parents could never have imagined.

■ Be prepared for the possibility that the younger generation may be better equipped than you are to handle certain areas of growth and change.

Parents who are not prepared for their children's ideas for growth and expansion inevitably run into problems. Explains one father, "I had my daughter meet customers, she went out, I went out with her, she spent a lot of time on the phone, she had great ideas for advertising and how to develop and expand the business. Little by little, I began to see that she was doing things I had wanted to do and didn't have the time to do and she did them so well that I became envious."

■ Confront new technology together.

New computer systems, phone systems or fax machines, for example, may or may not have a valuable place in your business. Evaluate your needs, make up a realistic budget for such changes and then make your decision together. Of course, there may always be differences of opinion, but if children can show the advantages of making such purchases, even parents who won't or cannot comprehend the new technology should not be unwilling to make them.

"When I came out of school, there was a lot of high-tech, very modern equipment," says one son, "and my father didn't want to buy any of it. And probably one of the things that made the practice successful was that I insisted on having all this," he says, pointing around the room to various machines and supplies. "Even though he hated it."

■ Be patient with your children's dreams, no matter how crazy they sound.

You too once had some growing up to do, so take a look back and try to remember who you were at your child's age. As one father points out, "My personality is not like my father's, who founded the business, but I see myself in my son. I'm watching him, with his grand ideas, and I see myself at his age."

Tips for Children on How to Handle Growth and Change

■ Proceed slowly.

It takes at least a year or two, possibly more, before the pace and tempo and cycle of any business can be fully appreciated—how orders are filled, bills are paid; how products are manufactured or made; how customers are contacted, follow-ups are made; how business relationships are established. You need at least that much time before you have the proper perspective to assess areas that could benefit from change.

■ Respect your parent's hard work and accomplishments; don't march in and expect to change things just for the sake of change.

There's the story of the father who worked every day of his life from five o'clock in the morning to four o'clock in the afternoon, making a living at his own business, which allowed his children to attend college and then medical school, business school or wherever they wished. And when the business-school graduate arrived on the scene, he told the father he was doing it all wrong, that the business needed more employees, better hours, new supplies, new computers—changes that amounted to hundreds of thousands of dollars. Looking over their finances, the father simply pointed to the bottom line in profits and said they would literally be out of business with such a plan.

■ **Strive for excellence in what exists before you push to expand.**

Focus on existing areas that need improvement—sales methods, services, product quality—before you divert attention too far afield into other ventures. "I said first I want to be as professional a company as we can be," explains one son. "I want to be in the forefront of fashion and industry and be the best. Constantly innovating, constantly being the company people want to imitate."

■ **Do your homework.**

If there is some piece of equipment to buy, area to be expanded or department that you feel would really benefit from change, put your case down on paper and back it up with facts and figures before you make your pitch. When a general agreement to make the changes you want has been reached, before proceeding with any plans, go over the details of what happens next—who will do what, how the business will be reorganized, how money will be spent, and so forth—so that you will continue to agree along the way.

■ Build support for your ideas from employees whose views your parent trusts.

One son went out to call on customers with his father's most experienced sales rep and came back with a well-documented estimate of potential sales orders for a new line of goods he wanted to develop. His initiative—and the feedback confirmed by the sales rep—so impressed his father that he gave his son the go ahead.

■ Don't give up immediately if you meet with a negative response, if you believe your ideas for the growth of the business are valid ones.

"Every once in a while, when the logic is there, he'll agree with some idea of mine. A shadow of a doubt, though, and I end up losing," claims one son.

Another son, who was shot down by his father after proposing a carefully thought-out plan for franchising, would not quit because he felt franchising was the key to the future. It was, but he had to go back and do more research to convince his father the start-up costs were worth it, and that they would not lose quality control by branching out. In the end, father and son reached a compromise. They would franchise the least profitable of their operations, and if it succeeded, they would proceed with the son's plans. The son was willing to risk his entire plan on the success or failure of one outlet, and the risk paid off. Sales tripled, and the family went on to focus their attention on the franchising of outlets for their product. In their case, franchising has also given the father a chance to share his professional experience—his mistakes as well as his successes—by personally training each new franchise owner. It is a job he never would have had the chance to do, and one that he particularly relishes.

In another situation, licensing became the issue. When the son proposed to his mother that he pursue a lucrative licensing arrangement, she reluctantly approved. When her son completed the deal in less than four months, all she could say was, "I can't believe you did that already." She was shocked but also very pleased.

> ■ If you run up against solid resistance, pull back.

"I have my own ideas. Everything [my father] does is not exactly the way I would do it," concedes one son. "A lot of times, I wish I were doing my own things. But right now, I'm only twenty-four, and I'll have time for that."

MONEY

Since parents have more experience, and money must be handled carefully, this is an area where, to avoid conflicts and problems, they would be wise to take the initiative.

Growth and Change

Tensions about spending money are often closely linked with growth and change.

If you are lucky, everyone will share the same attitude about spending money, as reflected in what one daughter had to say: "None of us is that motivated to ever have to borrow money. If we have it, yes, we'll spend it. But if not, we don't ever want to have that whole problem of struggling to pay it back. Yes, I'm conservative, and probably I get my outlook from my dad."

More often, differences come up.

If, at the suggestion of your son or daughter, you decide to go ahead with spending money, even if you may not be 100 percent behind it, invest only what you can afford to lose.

Treat such an investment as if you were going into the stock market or to the racetrack. A small investment of money that will not make that much difference to the way you live or the success of the business, but given freely to test results, leaves no chance for hard feelings should the money be lost.

After one father agreed to put an idea of his son's to a test with financial backing, there was no conflict after the idea failed because the son saw that it wouldn't work, and the father was relieved that he didn't lose too much money. "Luckily I didn't invest it all. We put our feet into the water, and almost got them bitten off."

Go in, take the chance and if your investment is lost, consider it over and done with, never to be brought up again.

If you can't keep financial promises, don't make them. And whatever else happens, don't renege on them.

One son was constantly running up against this. "As my father got older," he explained, "he would give me more leeway, but then sometimes he would pull the money back. And I'd go in and say, 'How can you have done this to me?' " Time and time again he considered getting out of the business, but instead he simply waited and stayed.

Wages and Payments

You and your children should establish salary, raises and bonuses—as well as profit sharing, stockholder status and other perks—preferably before they officially enter the office.

"I don't want them to be beholden to me for money," says one wise father. "I don't want to manipulate them for the sake of the dollar. Yes, I pay them a particular wage, but even at this stage, I have more than enough for myself. And every deal that we're in, I bring them in as a full partner. In other words, we go into a lot of real-estate deals where I split it up between them."

While there is no set standard for making a financial arrangement, it should be discussed and laid out as clearly with your child as it would be with other employees. Some families work with lawyers to turn over all the finances to children; others pay them a straight salary that is competitive with similar jobs in the field, at least initially, and make increases as time goes on, but the key is to agree that the arrangement is fair. When in doubt, some experts say, pay them more than you think they are worth.

Inside Operations

Be open to some of their ideas on how to handle finances. Some parents, no matter how successful the business, still believe they are running a mom and pop operation, and nothing that happens will change their view. Reluctant to give up financial reins, one mother is deaf to the idea that her company needs to hire a financial expert. Finally, her son feels he is on the right track. "But, Mom," he says, "this is a twenty-five-million-dollar company. There's a lot of money going through and you've got to think of a lot of people who have been with us for years." He has not succeeded yet, but in time he is sure his approach will convince her to let go.

If your children are working in an area of the business that requires making decisions about how money is spent, work together to establish a realistic budget for operating expenses, and give them the authority for deciding on out-of-the-ordinary expenditures that may ultimately save money.

Give your children the opportunity to manage some aspect of company money and, as with investments, be prepared for them to make mistakes, even if they lose some money. If you keep an eye on what they are doing and stand by to offer advice, their mistakes should not be too expensive. Chances are they won't repeat them.

Work on budgeting, sales revenue and expenses together with an accountant. Look ahead with long-term strategic planning on how you will allocate money. The more you work together, looking at the overall standing of the business, the more capable and committed your children will be to sharing its leadership.

If you cannot see your way to spending money on new equipment, materials or projects they want, propose that a paid consultant be called in to evaluate the situation objectively—it will usually be money well spent.

In fact, bringing in professionals who can help suggest better ways of doing business, saving time (and thus money), is a worthy consideration. As one mother describes, "We have a public-relations/marketing woman who comes in once a month for a day, and she looks over what we're doing and suggests we try this or that. She points out areas we would never spot for being more productive, such as something as simple as never personally answering the phone between nine and eleven in the morning unless there is an emergency. And do you know what? Those two, totally uninterrupted hours are like eight hours."

Set a good example for your children about how you spend your money. Let them understand the balance between taking hard-earned money out to spend on yourself, and investing it back in to keep the business healthy.

Succession

Openly and frankly discuss how you envision money being handled in a succession plan, as well as how wills are to be arranged to cover each family member in the business. (See Chapter 10 for more on this subject.)

DELEGATING WORK

In businesses where personal contacts are very important, it is difficult to know who should represent the client when the son or daughter is new to the firm. When Richard came in to our literary agency, I was representing all of our clients. However, I gradually turned over to him some of the work I was doing for certain authors, and then little by little, if I was not available because of some trip or meeting, I encouraged them to contact Richard on any problem they might have, because he knew as much about their project as I did. This approach worked out well for everyone, and eventually Richard began attracting his own authors who also know that if he is out or away, they can talk to me. This is due in large part to having adjoining offices, purposely keeping our doors open, showing each other our mail, discussing business on a daily basis—all of which clearly enables both of us to keep up-to-date on the needs of our clients.

With new clients, we eventually reach the same arrangement—whichever one of us makes the initial contact will start working with the client, while the other gradually becomes involved. Sometimes clients come to us, and sometimes, if we feel they have the potential to write a good book on an interesting subject, we pursue them.

If an author I may have brought in to the agency eventually prefers to do business with Richard, I think that's great because it's just what I want.

Parents who have had years of running the business on their own may be made uncomfortable by the prospect of delegating work to their children. If your attitude is "no one can do it as well as I do," difficult as it is, once you bring in a son or daughter it is time to change. Don't kid yourself. You're not the only capable person in the world. Keep an open mind and listen to the younger generation. You might even learn something. Even if delegating work is difficult for you, don't stand in the way of your son or daughter who prefers to do so.

As one son explains, "My father would tell me to do something, I would say fine, and if I thought one of my assistants could handle it, I would ask them to do the job and it would get done. And when he realized someone else had handled the task, my father would call me and say, 'But I asked *you* to do it,' never quite understanding the value to my time of delegating work to someone else who was just as capable as I was to do it." Clearly, this was the father's problem and not the son's.

Be explicitly clear about areas of responsibility you are delegating.

"My father gave me responsibility for a whole new division, actually made me the head of it, and then when I did whatever I wanted he would cut it back and say, 'You can't do that.' And I'd say, 'But I thought I was in charge of this.' It turned out that what he meant was that everything I did was okay as long as he approved it."

This father probably hadn't thought through exactly what responsibilities he was delegating to his son, and even if he had, he should never have tried to take them back.

WORK HABITS AND APPEARANCE

Don't set rules about work habits or appearance for your children just because you follow those rules yourself. Let there be a relaxed feeling about how things are run. Being too strict will get you nowhere, as one father found out.

"We are not in a high fashion district," he described, "but I wanted the women to dress for work. When my daughter walked in, before I knew it, they were all in jeans. And we had a big to-do about it, and we argued. To this day, they still wear jeans. I am the type who wears a tie even if I'm taking out the garbage, but as long as the work gets done, I don't find it so terrible anymore that women walk around in the office in jeans."

When Richard began coming into the office wearing blue jeans—something that I found inappropriate—I did not make a big deal about it. In fact, I learned to accept it, and it was Richard himself who started to realize that when there were important people to meet or appointments to go to, blue jeans were the wrong clothes to wear. He observed how I dressed on such occasions and had the good sense to follow my lead, without my telling him a thing.

Similarly, just because you may be an early riser and in the office by eight-thirty in the morning or earlier, it doesn't mean that your children should feel compelled to be in at that time. If they come in at nine-thirty because it is more comfortable for them, fine, and if they do hold things up by arriving later, most likely they will be smart enough to decide on their own to come in earlier. Leave it up to their discretion and their good sense of what is best.

Some parents feel they are entitled to certain privileges, for example, coming into the office a bit later than their children. "At this stage," concedes one father, "I don't come in at nine o'clock because I work out at seven o'clock in the morning. I feel that I've earned it. They haven't earned it. So let them earn it." This is fine, as long as they know they eventually will.

For every family, there will be many areas in which individual habits will differ. If I eat lunch in the office when I do not have an outside lunch date or appointment, it doesn't mean that Richard has to do the same. If he feels like going out and having lunch and spending an hour or an hour and a half relaxing at lunchtime, fine. It shouldn't bother you if your children do what is comfortable for them, as long as they realize—and most of them will—what it is they have to accomplish in the business.

You can set an example for your children of being an earnest, professional, hard worker in the office. "Sometimes you tend to slack off in the office because it's a family situation and you think you can get away with not being professional," explains one daughter, "but my father expects me to be very professional, and that's been a good experience." Don't push your way of doing things on your children. Be patient. Let them accomplish everything that they have to, in their own way. This is the one approach that proves right over and over again, despite how you might feel.

Says one father: "I don't like her work habits to this day; I prefer more structure, but she's very, very talented. Not only does she have a business mind, she's just super with people."

"She's not as well organized as she thinks she is, but that's going to come with time," observes another father. "She's right on track. She's embarking on getting to know people and she's doing that very well, because that doesn't go fast. Four years, five years—it takes time to get that."

These parents show great wisdom in allowing their children to make their own accomplishments, in their own way.

PERSONAL LIFE AND PRIVACY

While it is infinitely satisfying when children share their parents' commitment to the business, chances are there are other areas in their lives that are equally important. Personal relationships that may progress to marriage, choices about starting a family—these are all part of the normal course of a happy, healthy adulthood that vie for their time. It's true in any business, but when work is a family business, keeping personal life separate from business often becomes an even greater challenge and may even lead to conflicts.

"Problems came up," explains one father. "At first my daughter would spend five days with me in New York, but then she met a man who lived in Washington, D.C., and would fly down there on weekends. Then he moved up to New York and after they got married, she didn't want anything to do with me or work on the weekends. For us it became an impossible situation because when I would call her at night, rehashing what happened in the office during the day while she was out with customers, we started to rub each other a bit—what had been fine in the beginning was suddenly too much business and no family."

Had this parent and his child talked about the situation and reached some compromise, they probably would have avoided the problem, but for this and other reasons, their work relationship did not work out. But yours can if you:

■ Respect each other's personal life, and back off from discussing work-related topics off the job if you sense either of you prefer some distance.

■ Encourage your children to develop their own lives separate from yours and from the business.

■ Stand by ready to help with their personal life when they ask, but aren't nosy about it when they don't.

■ Encourage your children to develop a life separate from business, and encourage them to take vacations— real vacations that do not involve the business.

UNEXPECTED UPHEAVALS

While it is almost impossible to adequately prepare for personal crises or unexpected situations, maintaining a calm attitude that is free of blame can turn a catastrophe into a chance to develop closer family ties.

After the real-estate market became soft, one father candidly admits, "As a company, we're not doing as well as we used to. But fingers aren't being pointed, either. We're trying to pull together as a team to get out of this little mess, and move on to the next case and try to hit the upswing when it comes."

Another father's experience illustrates how demanding more of family members during personal crises can sour the work relationship. "I had a heart attack a little over five years ago, and when I was in intensive care for a month and out of circulation, my daughter did a fabulous public-relations job, calming our customers and telling them everything would be all right. She would visit me in the hospital and I would ask her every day how it was going, and she'd tell me it was fine, and it was. But when I finally did get up and back to the office, I found that I wanted to nitpick because I felt I had lost control. When perfection was expected, I would say, 'Now where was she not perfect?' "

He realized his mistake only after his daughter left the business. Don't you fall into that trap.

Children experience their own stage-of-life crises. One son describes the point after about five years in the family business when he considered leaving, taking his family to a city far away and establishing a business on his own. "It suddenly seemed very appealing but also important to me to gain the experience of starting up a business that only my father had. He set up his own business, and the success and failure and all the systems since have been dependent on him. To create something and see it blossom—well, I never had that. When I got here, everything was in place.

"My folks were obviously not that happy about my doing that, they wanted me here. And then for a number of reasons, I worked it out that I would stay. I would sort of redouble my energies here and see if we couldn't turn this into a more successful place. And that's what my work challenge would be. I could say to myself, 'Maybe I didn't make my own business, but I turned us from this successful into that successful.' Or helped do that. That's the direction we've been taking, and it turned out to be a good thing."

The divorce of one's parents can catapult a grown son or daughter into an unusual, very delicate position when parents are business partners. I once read a *Wall Street Journal* article about what happened when a couple separated and put their twenty-year-old son in charge of the day-to-day operations of their failing company. Focusing on the troubled business rather than his parents' personal situation, the son knew that in order to turn things around, he'd have to take drastic steps. He cut up his parents' credit cards and fired his sister and, in two years, through a carefully orchestrated strategy involving franchising, had increased sales sixfold and revamped the whole organization. In his own words, "You have to decide what you want to do, and do it. You can't get emotionally involved." The family has been behind him all the way; he's even rehired his sister to work in a position he feels she's better suited for than the one she previously held.

This situation is a good example of what I think is the best advice in a crisis situation: to put the most capable family member in command and give him or her free rein to exercise authority.

While it is very difficult to separate family problems from business affairs when you have a small business and are working closely together, the business must come first when such problems occur. If the business can remain intact and stay on course to grow, it will reward the members of the family after their problems are resolved.

When the upheavals involve conflict between family members, the person in charge of the business should make the decisions while keeping both sides of the family aware of what is going on.

If necessary, bring in an attorney or arbitrator to explain to all concerned the importance of keeping the business intact, rather than allowing it to fail because of a family conflict. The arbitrator might even be a respected mutual friend who can speak to both sides of the family to let them know what is best for the business. Perhaps each side would listen to the person more attentively than they would to someone within the family.

When there are upheavals, time proves to be the greatest healer. While the two sides might be really angry and not speaking to each other, in time, they may forget why they were so angry. An arbitrator may allow a family to work out problems in a normal fashion during a critical period.

Do everything you can to anticipate and prevent potential conflicts before they arise. When handling age-related issues and other potential problems, keep the following in mind:

■ Bring differences out in the open.

Don't let bad feelings grow by holding them in. Never allow a conflict to remain from one day to the next without addressing it, working on it, solving it.

■ Communicate with each other on everything that pertains to work.

Schedule regular meetings for this purpose, but also use "dead time"—traveling to and from meetings, for example— to discuss work-related problems. Consider planning business retreats. "Once a year, we go away with our accountant who's done this type of thing, and we talk about each department, about financial matters, about the goals of the company," explains one son.

■ Choose your battles.

"There was a lot of conflict as to what we should do and how we should do it," explains one son, "and most of the time my father would defer to me, but when he had a strong opinion on the subject, I would defer to him. I didn't want to be a winner in that situation."

"I know where I can win, where I should fight and where I shouldn't fight," comments another son. "I'm very good at saying, 'If this is the way it's going to be, let me go on and work around it.' And when I am outnumbered, I back off."

Both parents and children should be willing to back down when one or the other feels strongly about an issue.

In other families, for example, the parents defer to their children. "Most of the time when we come to some strong disagreement, I just do it my way," explains one son. "I just do it. Really, it's the truth. And I get the feeling that in the back of his head, he's thinking, 'What the heck is he doing now?' But somehow he says to himself, 'Look, let him do it. It's not worth the argument.' "

■ Be ready to admit you are wrong.

To resolve conflicts, one father explains, "It all depends on how stubborn each party is. There's got to be some give. It's like a marriage. You know, people fight, and they can wind up divorcing. It takes a lot to say you're sorry, and it takes a lot to admit that you were wrong. And if you are father and son, no matter who's wrong, somebody's gotta say they are."

■ Keep emotions out of business disagreements.

Keep the issues on center stage until they are resolved, and don't let feelings get in the way of solving them.

"It's the only way," admits one son, "because no matter how much you try not to be father and son, it always has a way of coming out. That's what you have to try to avoid."

■ When a disagreement has been resolved, let it go.

"We could stop after a big argument and be friends," one son explains.

Comments one person in a business with several family members, "A lot of times, in the heat of work, you may say things you regret—lose your temper, which is normal for all of us. Everybody has a bad day once in a while, but we're all old enough and wise enough to know that sometimes what's said in the heat of work doesn't really matter. It doesn't come from the heart, it comes from the guts. And we brush it off and forget about it in five minutes."

■ Don't try to force your opinions on others to get instant results. Whatever the issue, give it time.

As one son realized, in many businesses it can take years before your opinions really count for something. "The tendency is to come in and think that just because you have a fresh attitude, you are the only one capable of improving things. 'These guys have been doing the same thing for fifty years,' you think, 'and they're not millionaires; they must be wrong.' Well the point is, they're much more right than wrong. Just to keep a business floating is difficult enough, much less making money at it."

Some parents are not ready to let go, or even to delegate. "I'm the father of the family; they listen to me. I organize everything and they help me. As for stepping back and letting them come in to do what they want with their own ideas—not yet." When a parent feels that strongly, incoming family must be tactful and patient.

■ Don't withhold your opinions or valid suggestions.

Don't be timid about saying what is on your mind. Trust that others have the capacity to listen. When you make suggestions, make it clear that you have an opinion, but that you are reasonable about it. "You learn by listening to your folks and sharing their experience," one son suggests, "but when they know you've got opinions, eventually they listen too."

Explains another son, "When [my father] felt strongly about something and I disagreed with him, I would say to him, 'There are two ways of doing this; yours is no more right than mine. Why not let me try my way?' Even if I didn't get my way, at least I spoke up."

■ Use outsiders as buffers.

A mutually respected, trusted consultant—lawyer, accountant, whoever—can be used as a sounding board to provide an objective opinion when you are unable to resolve a problem. This approach is particularly valuable when the issue involves money.

At the same time, trust your instincts. Outsiders do not know your family nearly as well as you do, and sometimes that can lead to misjudgments. In one case, the son so convinced the accountant with his argument for expansion that when the accountant took it to the father, he told him he'd be crazy not to go ahead with it. But the father knew his son excelled at selling ideas, and he found vital areas where his son's plan had not been fully researched.

8 Bringing In Siblings

This chapter presents skills for maintaining a good solid rapport when the work relationship shifts from parent/child to parent/children.

In some families, the prospect of siblings coming into the business is seen as a natural progression; in others the very idea stirs up a whole flurry of issues and questions:

- Is there really room for all of us? For all concerned to get their fair share of responsibility and money?

- Am I prepared to work with my brother or sister?

- Am I ready and willing to work with two or more of my children? To treat them fairly, as individuals?

- What happens when one of my children is better as a manager than the others?

- Can we all get along? What about sibling rivalry?

- Will my sister or brother and I eventually be able to manage the business without our parents?

While all these are challenging issues, some of them never come up, and those that do are by no means insurmountable.

Based on the experiences of families who have thrived as their numbers on the payroll have increased, there are many ways parents can take the lead in bringing siblings smoothly into the business—if they want to.

ADVANTAGES AND REWARDS OF WORKING WITH SIBLINGS

Brothers and sisters working together can make their business relationship positive and productive. The following are some examples of the positive results of working with siblings.

■ An increased number of ideas and perspectives.

"There are four different personalities here," explains one brother, who is running the family business with another brother and two cousins. "That's good in a way because you don't want to hear the same thing. We all have different fears and concerns . . . we all leave our imprint on the business."

■ An increase in complementary talents.

"I'm a deal junkie," says one brother, a broker who thrives on competition.

"And I'm the one who worries about the checks coming in," describes his calmer sibling, who handles their company's finances.

■ <u>An increased, committed workforce.</u>

"As I told my father," comments one daughter who works with her brother and father, "our whole problem with this business is that he didn't have six kids to bring in instead of two."

"If there were more of us," says another, "they'd probably be in here also. There's plenty of room and plenty of work."

■ <u>New incentive to maintain high standards.</u>

Call it sibling rivalry or peer pressure at home, but in business, brothers and sisters motivate each other to meet challenges and do their best. "None of us has wanted out because I think we really enjoy what we're doing," says one brother. "We're very hard on each other. We try to establish high standards."

THREE BASICS FOR BRINGING IN SIBLINGS

To help establish a good working relationship, consider these three basics:

■ <u>Confirm that the other children really do want to join the business.</u>

Again, you cannot push. "Our older brother worked for my father for three years but he never wanted to be in the business," says one son. "He was forced into it by my father, and three years ago, he left."

With some siblings, there is never any question about

coming into the business. Some family members will seek other careers and don't consider joining the business, as was the case with my son David. Another possibility is that all of the children in a family want to come in, one by one, as soon as they are ready, which might not always follow birth order. Older siblings may change their minds about a chosen career, for example, and decide to come in and work with the family where a younger brother or sister is already solidly established in the business. On the other hand, one younger brother describes how he changed his mind about coming into the real-estate firm his father had started with his brother.

"I had too much pride," he says. "I couldn't have come in as a full partner from school because I was too green. If Dad had been alive, I would have worked for him. But an older brother? No."

After personal hardships and the experience of salvaging a foundering company, he decided to reconsider—"just to have something to do" until he got his feet back on the ground. It did not take long for him to realize that his previous work experience enabled him to bring "a new point of view to the business"—one that prompted him to stay and form a thriving business partnership with his brother.

Sometimes a trial run has a different outcome. "One of my daughters worked here for about two years and decided it wasn't for her," explains one mother. "And my son also worked for us for about two years, but he did not like being on the inside. He's in another field, but he still does a lot of brainstorming with us and gives us a lot of good ideas."

There are many variables that affect whether siblings come in and/or decide to stay in. Often their decisions depend on relationships within the family. Siblings who don't get along outside the family business will probably not get along at work. How parents treat each individual within the context of work, and how different skills and talents are applied to meet the goals of the business, also affect sibling work relationships.

■ Determine whether the business can support more family members and their dependents.

If the business, in its present state, cannot support additional family members, the door should not automatically be closed to those who want to come in. One family realized that they would have to expand the business if they were all going to make a living from it, and in their case the plan they decided on paid off. In this family, the parents first provided for the stock transfer so that their four sons would not be hindered by it. Then they gave their children the authority to expand the business where they thought it needed to be expanded. Their expansion plan ultimately put the business on an international scale and each of them has made a very comfortable living.

■ Determine competence and establish compatible goals.

Evaluate the job potential of siblings before they are hired, as with any other employee. This includes their ability to work with each other. Brothers and sisters must be ready to put sibling-related rivalry or conflicts aside, if they exist, and work together toward the common success of the business. "It's not a matter of who's number one or who's number six, or who gets his name in the newspaper," states one brother who runs a very successful restaurant in Manhattan. "It's the family name that matters. We're lucky that we always got along well, at play and at work, but what matters is not so much family, but who comes in the door. That's the most important thing here, that they are happy when they leave."

"Striving for perfection is something we all do intuitively, in each aspect of the business we are in," considers another sibling of the objectives he shares with his brother.

If there is genuine enthusiasm for the business, if there is room to accommodate everyone and if business goals are compatible, it is conceivable that any number of brothers and sisters can make a career of working together. With these initial considerations addressed, let's examine how typical families have handled some of the issues raised at the opening of this chapter.

TREATING CHILDREN AS COWORKERS

Parents need to make it very clear to siblings before hiring them that their ability at the job precedes family obligations, and that if the ability isn't there, they'd be much better off establishing a career elsewhere. One father explains, "I told my sons at the onset that each person who comes in has to make his own way. He's got to generate enough business to cover what he takes out of it."

Once your child is hired, it becomes more and more difficult to be objective in evaluating ability, and to cope with inability. The earlier you present a clear job description, and the ground rules for managing it, the better.

Treat all your children according to who they are, not as you wish them to be. Don't try to change their ways to suit your needs, but focus on directing their strong points into the business. "Even if one of them is more headstrong," suggests one father, "you've got to take it the way it is. You can't change people, even your children. Weigh what you've got, and try to make the best of it."

One father, in a business previously dominated by men, treats his daughter with such equality she sometimes feels she's the son he never had. "I am amazed at how fair he is," she comments.

If things do not work out, each member of the family must be willing to accept the consequences. In one instance, where his children's arguing got so out of hand that no solutions could be found, the father finally realized that having his oldest son in the business would never work. "You've got to leave," he explained to his son, "because if you stay here, I'm going to have a heart attack." The fact that the parent got along with his younger son, who skillfully controlled his temper at work when things got out of hand, did not enter into this father's decision. The decision to ask his elder son to leave was based solely on the unproductive relationship he had with him.

Firing family is surely one of the worst-case scenarios in a family business. The best way to avoid it, of course, is not to hire dubious candidates for the job in the first place, and/or to spell out very clearly up front what the requirements will be and to hold to them. If family members who are unsuitable for the job are kept on, the business and the individuals involved will usually suffer. Performance reviews can help buffer relationships between individual family members and prepare the way for a firing, but the business should always come first. If firing becomes inevitable, in almost all cases it is best done by someone outside the family.

DIVIDING THE MANAGERIAL PIE

As more family members come into the business and the balance between generations shifts, division of work and responsibility becomes a matter of greater and greater urgency. "As you grow," describes one father, "as more and more family members come in, you have to decide, 'How do you want to operate your family business?' And if it's everyone doing everything, there is going to be a conflict of interests because with everyone having different ideas, you'll start getting on top of each other and you'll fight."

Divide is the key word. "You've got to operate as a normal business," one brother suggests, "with everyone having their own responsibility." One restaurateur explains how his operation is divided. "My brother, my sister and I are in the front with customers. In the back, my two cousins are the chefs. Those are the strategic spots in the restaurant, and in each of those spots, we have our family."

"Everybody is pretty much segregated in their own department, so there's not a lot of stomping on toes," explains one brother. His sister adds, "We once worked in the same office—for about two weeks!"

"The way we work it out," says one brother, "and I think one of the reasons we've survived where other companies tend to feed on themselves and get into family conflicts, is that we've divided up the areas of responsibility. It's one company, but each division is separate."

How are divisions determined? In many families, brothers and sisters discover or stake out their own territory in the business. In one instance, with her younger sister already in place as the corporate leader, the older sister came in on a test basis and immediately gravitated to the one-on-one relationship with customers in the showroom, and to public relations. Such division of labor was ideal, as the younger sister explains, "because as all my duties and chores and obligations grew, it was more difficult for me to spend so much time out there in the showroom." They have neatly divided day-to-day responsibilities, but they also work together in a group that includes their father and a trusted nonfamily manager.

In another business, one son is president, the administrative leader who also directly supervises the operations management; the other is in sales and marketing, directing contacts with the company's selling representatives around the country and the two men in the sales department. "It wasn't initially decided who would do what," explains one of these brothers. "The reason it worked is that we have different talents. It happens we have enough room to do whatever we want to do. Fortunately, we gravitated to what we enjoy, and it's worked out well."

While siblings are free to work among themselves to find their own niche, parents cannot assume it will just happen. One father explains why he could never step back and say, "I'm content; you guys do whatever you want because eventually it's going to be your business ten or fifteen years down the road." Because of the personalities involved, he carved out what each son would do, and is himself clearly the leader. "Every day I say, 'What's happening here? What'd you do wrong? What'd you do right? Let's see what's going on.' It keeps them moving, keeps them rolling if I keep on them."

"I try to keep them apart as much as possible so that each one works in their own area," another father says of his children.

One daughter, in the business with her two brothers, comments, "Thank God my father had the foresight to give us each our own domain to run. We don't trip over each other's feet, and yet we all interlock in the end. We bounce everything off of everybody. Nobody is the big cheese; nobody is my boss, nobody is their boss. We each have our own little thing to run, all of which commingle, and it works very, very well."

One brother explains his work relationship with his brother. "What's different between our situation and many others is that our father has relinquished a lot of control and we can do whatever we want. And the reason it works is that we do different things. We don't get into each other's hair, we don't need to compete. We have our own problems in the areas we run."

Obviously, when work between brothers and sisters is clearly divided, conflicts are less likely to occur. But what happens when the market changes, the business moves in unforeseen directions and responsibilities become blurred?

This was the case in a commercial real-estate firm, where what started out to be neatly separated areas began to collide. "We're heading more into the lending area because we find there's not that much to buy that makes sense," explains one brother, "and she [his sister] is getting more involved in lending. It happens that this is my area of expertise, and just today we had a little conflict." This brother and sister were able to work out their differences, but, explains the sister, "if the little pep talks between us that we're all in this together, and we're all on the same side" had failed, they would have asked their father to step in as arbitrator.

What happens if fighting gets out of control?

"That's a very good question," reacts one gentleman, who owns a successful restaurant in Manhattan equally with his five sisters and in-laws. "That's the most difficult thing. But being that it is sisters and brothers, you just look back at your parents and the good things about the past and you think, 'Would they like for me not to make it in the business because of this fighting?' And at that point, you think it would be a good idea to revise everything and try to get together." In this family, with no parent in the picture, the loyalty to immediate family and the good memories of the past play a big part in resolving conflicts.

If children show themselves to be unable to resolve their squabbles or if parents are called in to mediate often between them, once again it does not bode well for the future and may eventually tear the business apart. If all of the family members do not eventually settle down into a harmonious work team, it would probably be smart to either liquidate the business or break it up into separate companies for each child. Otherwise, the battles waged after the parent is gone might very well break up an otherwise successful business that has taken years to build up. Disappointing as it may be to dissolve family connections in the business, if those connections are beginning to destroy the business, it is more important that the work, effort and time you put into it should continue under the guidance of someone outside the family.

INITIATING COMMUNICATION BETWEEN SIBLINGS

Parents who initiate regular family meetings can provide room for siblings to pool ideas, check on what the others are doing and, if need be, clear the air. "The main tool I've tried to use outside of daily contact and discussion is that we lunch together about once a month at a nice restaurant," explains one father. "We discuss the business, family squabbles, in an atmosphere that promotes keeping everything under control. And then if we want to discuss some details of the business, we go to some coffee-shop–type restaurant to talk about it. But the aspect of going to a fine restaurant—rising to a higher level, getting dressed up—the symbolism is extremely effective and we try to do that regularly."

Another parent concedes, "I think it would help if we had general meetings more often, just to air our feelings about what everyone is working on." In addition to the regular meetings this family has once a month to discuss business details, they plan to take periodic weekend trips as a group to discuss personal relationships in the business.

It's important for parents to help keep siblings apprised of what the others are doing at work, something I am especially conscious of with one son right here in my office and the other living in Florida.

BALANCING TALENTS AND ABILITIES

In most businesses, as described earlier, brothers and sisters seem to work best together when they can take on different areas of responsibility, according to where their talents lie. But what happens when one sibling is a better manager than the others?

After their father's sudden death, the status quo of two brothers who had beeen working on a more or less equal basis changed drastically. Without their father, the younger and more aggressive son was compelled to step forward as the prime decision maker and leader. He had to if the business was to move ahead. He was named president by his mother, in a move that has been very difficult for his older brother to accept.

"If I were older, it would be easy," explains this newly appointed president. "But he never said he was in charge of this, or he was in charge of that; and he never tried to fight for anything. Still, it was very, very tough for him. Everybody knew I was running the show, and that I was doing everything, and so this just confirmed it. I try to help him and encourage him, but he also knows me, and he knows my aggressive style, and he knows how I push to get things done."

The bottom line is clear: You do what is most expedient for business. If one sibling is better than another at managing, putting him or her in the leadership role simply needs to be done. In the words of the mother who did so, "There was no other choice."

In those cases where parents recognize that one child is better at making decisions than the other, the parent should ensure as soon as possible that the decision maker not be hampered or held back by the less qualified sibling. One solution, devised by a family business consultant, is to set up two classes of stock in the business: one voting and the other nonvoting.

As reported in a *Manhattan,inc.* feature on the Forbes family, Malcolm Forbes initially gave each of his five children an equal share of 20 percent of the company and changed their shares when they became adults so that the eldest son, Steve, who of all of his siblings was deemed most capable of taking over the reins from his father, would inherit 51 percent, an amount that would provide him with control of the company. Of his decision to revise the equal status of his children, Malcolm, Sr., was quoted as saying, "The quickest way to lose a family business is to have it divided equally among all its heirs."

It takes courage and maturity for parents and siblings to make business decisions that involve each other, and it takes acceptance on the part of the siblings who must defer to leadership of their brothers or sisters. When Steve Forbes was appointed heir apparent to his father's role at *Forbes* magazine, his brother Kip was quoted as saying, "With us, Steve is clearly the most capable," adding that it would be better for the company to have one man calling the shots than to have the power shared by "two very bright men with different opinions about how to run a business." In fact, each of Steve's siblings has fared well—brother Kip, as vice-chairman of the magazine; Robert, handling the Forbes family real estate; Tim, as president of *American Heritage* magazine, now a Forbes imprint; and sister Moira, although outside of the family business, working with disabled persons.

A recent *New York Times* article about the family-run Seagram Company described what happened when Edgar Bronfman, Sr., appointed the youngest of his three sons, Edgar, Jr., as president and chief operating officer of the company. In the article, the eldest son, Sam, conceded to being "chagrined" by his father's decision, while his uncle, Charles, co-chairman of the firm, openly disputed the plan. However, Edgar Bronfman, Jr.'s success in moving Seagram out of the dwindling liquor market and establishing it as a beverage company has shown the appointment to have been a wise one and, over time, one that his family has accepted.

DIVIDING THE FINANCIAL PIE

Despite differences in age or talents, when workload and responsibilities are divided equally, an equal financial partnership between siblings seems to be the fairest arrangement. In one family, there was a gap of fifteen years between the time when two older brothers joined the business and the arrival of the two younger ones. Despite the obvious issue of seniority, they decided they would all receive the same salary because they would all be doing the same amount of work. When a successor is named, leadership authority, in the form of voting stock or whatever, should clearly be spelled out in that person's favor.

When, for various reasons, responsibilities fall more heavily on one sibling than another, each brother and sister should be paid at least the average salary for their particular job, with benefits measured not by age, but by skills and assumption of roles. The family member who works exclusively on the loading dock, for example, should be paid the going rate for the job and, perhaps, be given a nonvoting share of stock in the company equal in value to voting stock. If possible, parents or nonfamily members of management should make these determinations and appointments.

OTHER WAYS IN WHICH PARENTS CAN ENCOURAGE SIBLING HARMONY

■ Prepare your children in advance for the prospect of working together in the business.

One father made a proposal to his children before any of them had positions in the business. "Some ten years ago, I said, 'You know, you all have assets. Why don't you start a family company for investments and see what would happen over a period of years?' And they did. And all of them [two brothers and two sisters] had to consult with each other and work with each other and plan with each other." The whole experience carried over to their interactions in the family business.

■ Be sure to give space to the children already in the business to air their views and ideas about brothers or sisters coming in.

Very often, children already working in the business may have ideas or suggestions that will help incoming siblings make the transition.

"I was a little apprehensive about my brother coming in," explains one daughter, "because originally he was going to join us right out of college. And I just didn't think that was right. I discussed it with my father, and he agreed with me, and my brother worked for someone else for about a year. And I think he's really happy he had that experience."

While it was not initially in his plans, the brother wholeheartedly confirms the benefits of working elsewhere first.

■ Let your children work out personal conflicts or rivalries between themselves; do not intrude unless they ask for advice or things get so out of hand it affects the business.

In the words of one parent, "I try to stay away as much as possible from their conflicts because with those kinds of things, it's better off if they work them out themselves."

"They may get into sticky situations," observes the father of three daughters, "but they have to work it out for themselves. They have arguments, they have opinions—but it all works out because they have open minds. If one says something, the other tends to say, 'Let me see. . . . You know, you are right.' They work it out together."

WHAT SIBLINGS CAN DO TO ENCOURAGE HARMONY

When asked if they fight at work, many siblings will answer "Not really, there's too much to do." And yet, when rivalries date back to their childhood years, some brothers and sisters have a harder time establishing a work relationship with each other than they do with their parents. Here are some guidelines siblings have used in working harmoniously together:

- Should conflicts arise, they should be kept out in the open.

- Small misunderstandings should be distinguished from larger ones.

- Observe and help each other on the job.

It is to everyone's advantage to work to stay together, stand up for each other. In hindsight, one brother, observing his father's effect on his older brother's performance, explains that, "My father would be very sharp and shoot my brother down, and my brother would be totally unable to make a decision because he couldn't handle the blame if something didn't go right. Partly because I just came in and did things, he was so relieved about not having to make decisions, that he didn't do anything."

Having made these observations, the younger son might have encouraged his brother and helped him to develop the skills to handle such problems with their father.

■ Keep some distance from each other in your private lives.

"We're each other's best friend and closest adviser," says one brother, "but we try not to socialize. That's always a problem in a family business. If you're together on Sunday, it's hard to be all business on Monday."

Says one sister, "My brother and I are very, very close, so I definitely separate the sibling part of our life from that of being business colleagues."

■ Recognize and accept each other's strengths and assets and, more important, don't try to use them to compete for parental attention or advancement.

"In the beginning, we felt our way along," explains one third-generation brother, "but it became obvious very quickly that my brother is very knowledgeable in our field, more knowl-edgeable than I in certain respects." With this basic under-standing, serious conflicts were avoided as these two brothers worked at finding their respective niches in the business.

"I know there are clients he doesn't get along with or I don't get along with, for one reason or another, and if the one of us they want isn't available, that's fine," describes one brother. "A lot of what we're doing involves developing a certain personal rapport and clients can come back later with neither of us having any hard feelings about it."

"My sister works more closely with my father," describes one woman. "She really tries to emulate him. But I don't see myself at all as a businesswoman—it's not me. And I think the combination is good. I'm more by nature a teacher, and I think that the differences between us give people more confidence in us."

Malcolm Forbes recognized his brother Bruce's contributions to the business. As quoted in *Forbes*, he says, "Bruce's unfailing zest and dynamic enthusiasm were key in raising our circulation [and the number of] our advertising pages. . . . He inspired unique loyalty. He got the ball rolling."

■ Compliment each other for a job well done— and mean it.

If there is genuine enthusiasm for the business, if there is room to accommodate everyone and if business goals are compatible, it is conceivable that any number of brothers and sisters can make a career of working together—provided there is true ability, talent and the desire to work harmoniously together. Before offering children a place in the family firm, parents should evaluate the potential of each child.

Work responsibilities, management authority and financial compensation should be clearly and fairly divided, according to talents.

The family business gives siblings a valuable opportunity to demonstrate maturity, to leave old conflicts in the past, if they exist, and to build a deeper, more rewarding adult relationship.

9 Making an Extended-Family Business a Success: Is There Room for In-laws, Spouses and Other Relatives?

The farther the members on the family tree branch away from the immediate family that started the family business, the thornier the boughs seem to become and the more problems are apt to occur. Of course, there are always exceptions—the even-tempered uncle valued for his leadership and ability to smooth out family frictions; the competent brother-in-law with a special skill that is essential to the organization; the cousin-once-removed whose marketing experience provides an unexpected money-saving management resource. With capable and compatible in-laws, spouses or other relatives who want to join in, making the business an extended-family business can be an ideal way to add needed skills or work service.

However, establishing a successful relationship in business with in-laws and other relatives, particularly those who are put in line for leadership, is the exception rather than the rule.

COMMON CHALLENGES TO BRINGING IN EXTENDED-FAMILY MEMBERS

■ Personal incompatibility.

If you roll your eyes at having to be in the same room with your brother-in-law at the occasional family gathering, chances are you will not relish his daily presence at work. It is notoriously harder to establish rapport with such a relative than it is with one's immediate family, because there is no longstanding sense of family loyalty to draw from to make an effort to get along at work.

"We have an account in Jersey," describes one son who is working in a family business, "and the brother-in-law came into their business and is starting to take over, and everybody hates him. Everybody—from the salespeople to the truck drivers who deliver for him. And it's a hindrance to their business too, because whenever you have to deal with them, it's usually with him because he is in a position of authority, and you take a dislike to him."

Although they have yet to face the in-law scenario, one brother, along with his sister, are in principle inclined to keep other relatives in their family out of the business. "We may have jobs that overlap," the brother comments, "but I don't know if she or I would bring anybody else in from the family. We have our own arguments, but we're brother and sister. If you're married into the family, I don't know, it's harder because you're not brother and sister."

■ Business problems.

If a problem occurs because of poor business conditions or some other reason that requires employees to be laid off, letting an in-law go might prove extremely difficult without suspicion of family favoritism. If you try to avoid that suspicion by letting nonfamily members be the first to go, you may lose an employee who is better for the business than your in-law. Because of these and other in-law dilemmas, it is important to think twice before bringing in-laws in, unless you are compatible in every way possible, and it's understood that the welfare of the business always comes first.

■ Jealousy.

Very often—too often—an in-law will be jealous of a son or daughter in the business. Many times, when the in-law leaves the business, he or she winds up taking away or stealing accounts or business from the people who gave them their start.

■ Incompetence.

Hiring spouses, in-laws and others on the basis of family kinship or obligations rather than competence is worse than picking employees blind. One father who works with his wife and son expresses the typical apprehension, and unspoken relief, that the problem of incompetent relatives never materialized: "If my daughters had married guys who had nothing to do and needed a job, my goodness, what would we have done then?"

Even if your brother-in-law is a well-intentioned, easygoing person whom everyone forgives for his mistakes, the business will inevitably suffer if he comes in and makes those mistakes at its expense.

HOW TO MAKE AN EXTENDED FAMILY BUSINESS A SUCCESS

Not all relatives are potential problem-makers, and the decision to bring them into the business does not always have to be an unequivocal no. The following criteria can help you determine whether or not to hire in-laws or other relatives.

■ Formulate and adhere to a policy decision about working with members of your extended family.

To ensure harmony within the immediate family, siblings and parents should discuss and agree among themselves whether or not to bring in relatives and, in particular, spouses.

One father explains why he and his children decided not to hire relatives. "The wives are not involved, and neither is my daughter's husband. Right or wrong, we felt that it would not be the right thing to bring the married couples into the business. Otherwise, you're really going to create a conflict. This way, it's all out front, the kids are in their own division, they're doing their own thing and there's great harmony."

It is far better to iron out differences about in-laws and other relatives before they come in. One son was so sure he could not work with his brother-in-law, who was more than qualified for the job, that the rest of the family let the brother-in-law go, sensing it would become a problem for all of them. Family members with reservations about bringing relatives into the business have an obligation to voice them, first by acknowledging their talents, followed by a

fair explanation of their possible drawbacks in the business.
A "trial run" when potential problems clearly exist is asking
for trouble. Where there are differences of opinion—as
when a son or daughter might want to bring in his or her
spouse and the other siblings don't—parents, or individuals
from the older generation, are probably best suited to resolve
the issue. "My father and my uncle were the ones who
determined that we try to keep our wives out of the business," states one successor, and so he and his brother did
just that.

In another situation, a father comments, "My daughters'
husbands all have their own careers, in other businesses.
This is what I wanted, and it's another reason why it works
out well."

Even where in-laws are in the business, when asked how
they feel about it, family members will counsel others against
bringing them in. Says one brother, who started a business
with his five sisters, who in turn each brought in a husband,
"I would say, stay out. No question about it. It's one-
hundred-percent better. They should be in their own business. And everyone I speak to," he adds, "says the same
thing." Apparently, one set of problems that commonly
crops up involves in-laws who have expertise in another
field, and who try to bring it into the family business in a
belligerent fashion. Contrary to his advice for other families,
this gentleman has managed to work with his five brothers-
in-law for the last thirteen-and-a-half years. In his situation,
not only does everyone have a separate area of responsibility
in the business, but each also operates with the same basic
understanding, that is, in this gentleman's words, "You have
to realize that you need to depend on the business to make
a living. You have a good reason to get along because with
the money you make in the business, you are bringing up
your family, supporting them, doing a lot of enjoyable

things—you make a decent living, and therefore you have a good reason to get along. Nobody is keeping you here. And if you want to be a real boss, you should be on your own. You don't belong in a group like this. This is an association; nobody is really the boss. We are all partners."

■ **Make it very clear to relatives what the line of succession will be.**

Settle the issue as early and clearly as possible, and you will avoid one of the most common and pervasive power struggles that occurs in a family business.

■ **Consider keeping the door open for part-time work.**

In some families, spouses are "a little bit in, and a little bit out," as one mother puts it. They support the family business when needed, and step out when not. Comments a daughter, "Mom's kind of like the revolving door—she comes in a few days, she goes out a few days."

"My sons are here with me every day, but my daughters-in-law only come in when I need them," is how the founder of one company worked out the problem. Since his business is seasonal, he is more than grateful to have spouses and extended family pitch in when needed. Nephews and nieces, even those who are not destined for succession, can provide manpower while getting valuable job experience by working in the family firm during summers.

In our own business, once in a while when our secretary is out of the office for a day or two for some reason, we call on my wife to come in and help out. She is only too glad to do so because it gives her a chance to contribute, as well as time to spend with Richard.

Having spouses or in-laws work part time can also give you a tremendous advantage in getting a different perspective on weak spots and ways to improve the business.

"When you are constantly in the flow of the business, and you go from one thing to another, sometimes you can't sit back and see the forest for the trees," explains one mother/boss, "which is what my husband can do for us, on the outside looking in."

In a field where men are known to negotiate many of the big decisions, this same mother does not hesitate to call her husband in to speed up decision making when negotiating crucial business deals. "There have been many changes and advances where women in the business have come a long way, have been recognized in the industry," she explains. "But there are still things that men would tend to leave vague with us if my husband weren't there. His presence has helped us a great deal in many of the areas where they would have taken longer to respond to our requests. Everyone comes right to the point and it's much more businesslike."

The presence of her husband was also critical early on in the business, when establishing credit was very difficult for women. "When we first started, we could not get a credit card for the company and I had to rely on my husband at that time," she explains.

If you take this route, just be clear in establishing where involvement begins, and ends. The part-time work situation may become a problem if it is defined too vaguely or too informally.

■ **View relatives as fair job candidates first, family second.**

Be candid and open with each other. Make it clear with relatives on the job or being considered for the job that the goal of working together must be one of mutual opportunity—not obligation. Explain how you envision succession to take place; who will be in charge. Let them know that their performance will be reviewed as fairly and as often as with other employees—family and nonfamily alike. By approaching the prospect of working together in this way, anyone in the family who wants to come in can be given the chance to do so. There are many instances where relatives may prove to be unexpected assets in the family business; be open to the possibility.

■ **Communicate about performance through nonfamily managers or through the family member closest to the relative.**

This is especially valuable when criticism is involved, as it is invariably easier to take from the relative/manager in the business to whom the person on the receiving end is most loyal.

One brother/manager explains how this works in his business. "My wife has been in here at times," he says. "She's very good at selling. As far as her status as an employee, to avoid ruining personal relationships, my brother and I have worked things out so if he wants her to do something, or change the way she does something, he tells me and then I tell her. That way, we avoid stirring up trouble."

■ **Be receptive to the opinions and suggestions of other, nonfamily employees about the relatives you bring in.**

Be fair. Put family ties aside so you can recognize who has the best abilities for a given job. These qualities instill respect in nonfamily staff and keep them from quitting when relatives are brought in.

Encourage nonfamily members to speak out and air their views about your relatives, even when they involve issues relating to job performance or compatibility. Often it is the nonfamily member who can provide accurate insights into weak areas of performance, as well as suggestions on how to improve them. Listen to your valued nonfamily employees, thank them for their candid input and use their observations when you evaluate and decide on how to handle a particular problem.

■ Confront conflicts one issue at a time, and work to contain them.

Show in-laws and other relatives that the immediate family really cares about resolving conflicts, that you'll let nothing continue unattended. Have the courage to discuss conflicts openly; isolate the problem and, if need be, get a nonfamily member to mediate until a solution is reached.

■ Be thoughtful and caring of family members who are not in the firm.

Through their family ties, spouses and close relatives, although not on the payroll, are ultimately still very much a part of the family business. Family members working together need to be especially aware of how their work relationship affects their most personal outside connections. Comments one daughter, "If you marry into our family and don't know anything about real estate, you're lost." Fortunately, this hasn't created a conflict, but it has still required careful thought and a constant awareness about not spending free time discussing work topics.

"We have to be very conscious of not monopolizing the conversation around our business," she explains. "Very conscious. I mean, if we go out to dinner with a client, it's okay. But if we're out to dinner with anyone else, one of us somehow will get onto real estate and if two of the family members are there, you can forget the rest of the table. We'll just sit and talk about the business."

"My husband has always been very helpful to me about the business, but sometimes he gets a little tired of hearing about it," explains another daughter. "I learned that because he's so smart and so interested, I can talk about business all the time. Which is something I've really had to learn to leave at the office, because otherwise we'd be talking and talking and suddenly he'd say, 'I don't want to be talking about this right now.' And I can understand that."

One daughter has her own plan for achieving a balance in her life. "I kind of look at all of life as a business, but with each part separate," she says. "You've got your business at home, with your husband and your children. You've got your business with your family, here at work. And you try to balance it out and make it all work."

Of course, you can't deny that a certain amount of work will come home—that happens with any job. However, when it's a family business, it seems to benefit relationships all around when a spouse's opinion or advice is limited to significant problems. "My wife loves it that I work with Dad," comments one son. "I think partly because it's rare I mention anything about work to her."

So while each family situation is different, be aware of how much you can discuss of the business without it being an imposition.

Also remember to keep in contact with your close family members who are not in the business. In some families, keeping parents, siblings, spouses and others who are outside the business from feeling neglected is an even greater challenge than keeping business topics from intruding, or monopolizing the conversation.

One father observed that because his sons work with him in business, they tend not to have as much contact with their mother. "I notice that while I call my mother in Philadelphia all the time, at least once a week," he explains, "my sons probably never call their mother because even though we don't talk about family at work, there's still a family attachment. I'm their parent connection, and they have less contact with their mother because I am in business with them, just as they'd have less contact with me if their mother were in here."

In our own case, I think my wife envies the fact that I see Richard every day, and she only sees him when he and his family visit us, or we visit them. It is up to the son or daughter in the business to keep up those contacts, with an extra call or visit if need be, so that members of their immediate family—brother, sister, mother, father—do not feel they are out of the picture.

If you are going to work at all with in-laws and other relatives, make it very clear that they will be judged just as any other employee—with no special privileges. Let them know they are coming into the family business just as they would any other business, and will be treated as other employees are.

Make it clear what their job will be, who they report to, how advancement will be determined.

Let relatives know who in the family you envision taking over—how you plan succession to take place.

If relatives you've hired reach a point at which they feel they are ready to go out on their own, don't hold this against them; otherwise, you just might end up creating a competitor. Let them know it is their privilege to leave; they have the same right as any other employee to do so.

Do not let the family business eclipse other valued family connections.

Keep up your contacts with close family members who are not in the firm.

Part Three

Succession

10 Planning and Implementing Succession

"Are we all going to fight when he is gone?" asks one daughter. "Are we going to have a problem?"

If the whole idea of succession fills you with fear and trepidation, you are not alone. Succession is perhaps the most vulnerable phase in family businesses. Between managing the related changes in finances and handling the potential conflicts, the odds of having succession go smoothly decrease with each generation. For founders to succeed in passing their firm on to their children is considered a triumph; for the business to make it through to the third generation, a miracle.

The prospect of one generation leaving and the next coming in to take its place is most foreboding to parents who have no intention of stopping their own work. For them, succession may imply forced retirement or cause personal turmoil of some kind. It is not only parents who become anxious about it; children have their own doubts and reservations. "Can I handle the pressure of keeping the family business going?" they ask themselves. "What if I mess up?"

If you find yourself wondering whether you really have to leave or, on the flip side, whether you really have to take over, this section of the book will confirm, through the advice and experiences of others who are managing to deal with succession, that it need not be a painful rite of passage. Succession can be handled as a smooth process designed to serve everyone's best interests: the business's, first and foremost, but also the interests of each family member involved.

There are three basic elements essential to a smooth succession process:

■ *Long-term planning.* A mutually beneficial succession may take anywhere from ten to fifteen years from the time the successor comes in. The more time spent grooming management for succession, the more solidly established your plan will be when the transfer of power occurs.

■ *Mutual readiness.* On the parent's part, this involves a willingness to share leadership and decision making; on the child's part, a willingness and an accumulation of skills needed to assume them.

■ *Flexible implementation.* This involves the completion stage of the transition of leadership—the older family members ceding top management positions to their children or other chosen members of the younger generation. Flexible implementation involves tailoring the process to the style of the individuals involved, and being open to changing it as the succession process evolves.

Each of these elements includes several areas and issues that are well worth considering in more detail.

LONG-TERM PLANNING

Whether you intend to stay on at work until you reach a ripe old age, or would leave tomorrow if you could, planning for succession as far in advance as possible will help everyone avoid unpleasant surprises. As you begin working together, you and your offspring should possess an awareness that together, you are ultimately working toward the goal of a complete transfer of responsibility from one generation to the next.

■ Discuss succession in a forthright, open manner, as early as possible.

"I always discuss the future with her," says one father, who is especially sensitive about succession because in his business the market is changing so radically that selling off might someday make sense. "I always discuss that with her. My father did not do that with me," he says, "and I always found that to be terrifying. To bring family into the business, and then to speak to somebody else about selling it? Terrifying. I had many fights with my father over that. Once he was negotiating with someone and I found out and told him he had no right to sell the business, that I could make it work. With my daughter, I would never think of doing such a thing without discussing it with her and getting her approval. I thought it was very cruel of my father to attempt to do otherwise."

Be candid with your children and other family members involved in the business about your own views on succession, including how you plan to choose a successor, if that's an issue. As the incumbent leader of the business, the plan may ultimately be the parent's, but because those who come next must live with it, all family members and other key employees should be encouraged to voice opinions and to contribute their own ideas.

Respect those opinions, whatever they might be. One daughter is very candid about being uncommitted, at least for now, to taking over her father's business. "I don't really think ahead that much," she says. "I think about now. I don't know what I want to do so far ahead. I feel very comfortable and secure in what I'm doing here, but right now I can't say this is it for the rest of my life. And yet if it is, I'm happy with it. I have a good feeling about it." For now, this is her prerogative, but the succession process should remain open to discussion.

■ **Determine who will take over.**

Ideally, this should be the parent's choice. If there is only one candidate for the top job, the matter is easily settled. However, if there is more than one child or another member of the family in the running, time will be well spent by holding off on a decision and observing job performances (and, perhaps, conferring with trusted nonfamily members of the firm) to determine who is most qualified. The only determinant should be talent—not birth order or the sequence in which individuals joined the business.

Once a choice has been made, share it with others in the firm as early as possible, particularly with those inner-circle family members who may have thought of themselves in line to take over. One of the worst ways to announce your choice for successor is to gather the pool of family-member candidates together unexpectedly and state your choice as a fait accompli.

Sometimes deciding on a successor among the younger

family members can be deferred, particularly if the top management position is shared by another member of the older generation. This was the case with one father running the business with his brother-in-law. Since three of the children were doing equally well heading up separate divisions of the company, they decided that if the father were to leave before a successor among them was chosen, the brother-in-law would take over and that by the time he left or retired, the natural leader among the children would have been determined.

■ Define the future position of key nonfamily management.

If nonfamily personnel are treated with respect and kept apprised of succession plans, there is no reason to expect that they will pick up and leave unexpectedly when it happens, which would obviously cause a nightmare for a son or daughter successor and deal a potentially lethal blow to the business.

To avoid that scenario, it makes good sense to determine well in advance with valued nonfamily members how they will be included in succession as you tell them about your plans. Working out advantageous terms and provisions for their future may involve the "golden handcuffs" approach, but bringing key employees into your discussions about the future is often all that's needed to demonstrate how much they are valued by the family and to keep them from jumping ship.

In one case, where the father has set a cut-off date for leaving his business and going on to a whole new career, the daughter, who will take over leadership, says, "There are other people here who are extremely capable—my father is not the only person. I think the reason why the company does so well is because of its people, and there are a lot of excellent supervisors here. I know the company can run without him; I really think it can, but I think all of us are really going to have to group together and take on a little more responsibility." This daughter is well aware of the value of nonfamily to the firm, and she will do everything she can to keep them on, beginning with open appreciation for their talents.

Plans for what to do about key nonfamily managers can even be made when and if children are undecided about their future in the business. Since it is not unheard of for family members to change their mind about coming into the firm after their parents are out of the picture, some business owners who turn top management positions over to nonfamily members of the firm will do so with a buy-sell agreement that includes a provision allowing children the option to buy out the key, nonfamily employees. The expense of providing for such a late-date deal may be worth it if your objective is to keep the business in the family.

■ Consolidate the financial picture.

Bankruptcy, just as often as conflict, accounts for a family business's failure to continue after the founding generation. Finances, trusts and estate planning—these are the areas where it really pays to seek the advice of a tax expert, accountant and/or lawyer. Plan ahead so that the family successors to your business are not ruined by the financial burdens of inheritance.

Unless it is a mom and pop operation with both parents deeply involved in the business when the children come in, the sons or daughters in the business should assume ownership after the parent who brought them in leaves.

I know one case where the sons told their father that if their mother came into the business, the two of them would actually walk out. Not that they don't love her; they do. But they knew well enough from their personal relationships with her that they just could not get along in business. Such situations can be difficult, but knowing his children's feelings, the father had to consider making an arrangement that after he was gone, his wife would continue to receive some income from the business—but with no direct involvement or ownership.

In another case, a father and son were working together in business and the father died unexpectedly without ever discussing finances with his son. It turned out that the stepmother, as beneficiary of the father's estate, had complete control of the business. Animosities grew so rapidly that within a year the son left to set up his own competing business and under the leadership of the stepmother, the father's business ultimately failed.

Any son or daughter who is not in the business should not be given a part of it when the parent/owner leaves; some other arrangement should be made. Siblings who are involved in the business should be the ones to divide up the company stock, while those outside should receive other assets, for example, a little income from the business if possible, or some other assets beside the business might go to them.

All of this should be openly planned and discussed, with the complete understanding of all parties involved. In most situations, estate planning and financial consolidation can begin around the time new members of the family begin working—even if you are planning to work together indefinitely. Include all parties who will be involved in future leadership in the financial discussions to determine the best all-around financial plan, and stick to terms voted on by the majority.

"There were thirty-nine trust funds involving my four children and six grandchildren; all of them had to be cleaned up in order to arrange our family company the way it is," says one father.

Many families reposition the financial picture so that children are given ownership of the business long before the parent leaves. Says one father, "Actually, I don't own this gallery. All four children own it. I just work here. And in order to work here, I provide muffins and bagels and cream cheese. I watch, and teach. They pay me the money they owe me." He can joke about it because it works out so well, but it took this family a full year with attorneys and accountants to make it a legal arrangement.

Sometimes the arrangement preferred by the parent is a gradual transfer of ownership. "He's given my brother and me a lot of his share of the business," explains one daughter. "He wants us to have it when we are young, and he wants us to learn what to do with it in the future. Not that it's just handed to us in later life, when I don't know what I have, or what to do with it, or how to handle the money. Slowly he gives us more and more each year, and he expects us to be able to make it grow. His parents treated him like that, and he is just passing it on."

If what this parent did appeals to you and you are counting on business assets as the source for your retirement money, set what you need safely away as soon as possible before turning the ownership over to your children.

In another situation, a father/daughter leadership team has recently worked out an employee stock ownership plan (ESOP), selling one-third of the business to their employees. "Down the road, I am gradually moving out of the business on a day-to-day basis," explains the father. "I don't get as much involved as our president or [my daughter], who together pretty much run the business day-to-day. That will probably continue. At one time I thought of retiring, but I probably won't. I have bought another business, and my daughter is getting involved with that one now. I'm also on another project which has nothing to do with this."

When Richard joined the company, it was my hope that it would work out, which it has, and that as the years went along he would get increasingly more money than I did from the business in order to support his growing family, and eventually would get full ownership and control of the business once I was gone. Other than that, I did not have anything else in mind at the time he came in. Not only has it worked out exactly as I envisioned, but as far as I am concerned, the business is now his, and I am just taking out of it whatever monies I need to be comfortable and enjoy my life. I am perfectly content with this situation, and in fact I hope it will continue that way until he takes it over completely, even though I predict that won't happen while I am still able to come in to the office.

■ Plan for future growth and change.

Creating a plan for change and growth is a succession imperative. The longer the outgoing generation is around to plan and be part of it, the more their children can absorb from their parents' years of experience. Since growth and change involve capital, the risk of losing money can be minimized by working together to decide what direction to take. Many times, children criticize the conservatism of their parents. They come into the business raring for change—

eager to start correcting their parents' "dumb mistakes." In time, realistically about five or six years later, they turn around and realize that their parents' way of doing things is just fine. In waiting for their turn to take control, ironically, when it is their turn, the children may do nothing at all. "I am going to run this business in the same way my parents did—that is, at the very, very high end of it. That's the niche my folks established, and it is a wonderful niche, difficult as it is. But I was trained in it, and grew up in it, and it is so natural to me that I don't think I could step down. I'd rather keep it where it is."

This is also how it is for Rich Snyder, the successor to his parents' In-N-Out hamburger chain in California. As reported in *Forbes* magazine, he is adamant about not tampering with the niche his parents carved out, claiming he will never change or add to the menu—or rapidly expand with new outlets on expensive real estate. Sons or daughters who hesitate to make abrupt changes in what their parents have done to keep the business going are usually the ones who demonstrate the maturity and wisdom required for top management decision making.

It may take time to tailor changes that will be needed to fill out any gaps that may occur when parents leave, particularly in those businesses that are built on the personal talents of the founding generation. In the case of a jewelry company where the mother was a gifted designer, or the custom furniture company where the father's designs were integral to the business, the first step in the succession process is obviously to find a substitute or alternative of some kind. In both examples cited, while many existing in-house designs were kept available, the emphasis gradually turned to the work of new designers. Naturally, much care went into the process, with the artist/parent participating in making the selections.

MUTUAL READINESS

Letting go, taking on—these are the omnipresent dynamics at the heart of the succession process in a family business, and on both sides they involve trust, confidence and skill. In almost every area of work that involves top management decision making, the willingness of both generations to engage in the transfer of responsibilities is the best gauge for timing the phases of succession.

How ready, willing and able are you, as a parent, to begin letting go? And children, how receptive are you toward assuming top management responsibilities? Use the following checklist, geared to elicit positive responses, to examine your attitudes about succession readiness.

Questions Parents Need to Ask Themselves

■ Do I listen openly to my successor about his/her plans for the business for growth and change? Do I encourage such dialogue?

■ Difficult as it may be, am I able to give over areas of autonomy to my successor?

■ Do I feel confident about his/her leadership abilities?

■ Am I able to take time away from the office without worrying and constantly checking in?

■ Have I imparted all I know about running the business to my successor?

■ Do I trust my would-be successor's judgment when it comes to handling, spending and allocating company money?

■ Have I openly championed the talents of my successor to our clients and customers? Allowed him/her room to deal with them without interference?

■ Have I planned the transfer of ownership and finances so it won't be a detriment to the business or the family?

Questions Would-Be Successors Need to Ask Themselves

■ Do I feel capable of managing this business?

■ Do I have enough experience to run this business?

■ Do I have a clear plan for how I would run the business?

■ Am I willing to take on as much responsibility for a project as my parents do?

■ Do I understand and respect my parent's way of managing the business?

■ Whatever stage of work I am in, do I willingly offer to take on more of the business and try to master it?

■ Do I seek out and initiate projects of my own, and follow through on them?

■ Am I able to seek out and listen to my parent's advice and comments on my performance?

■ Do I have the courage to risk criticism when I make my own decisions?

- If I am criticized, can I accept and evaluate criticism?

- Do I support the role and efforts of my sister or brother in the business? Do we work together as a well-balanced team?

- Do my siblings and I share a vision of family harmony in which, at the office, business comes first, family second?

FLEXIBLE IMPLEMENTATION

This is the completion stage of the planned transfer of top management positions.

You may already have thought a lot about it, or not at all, but sometime during the process of turning over the responsibilities of the day-to-day operations to successors, parents would be wise to consider their own future roles in the business by (1) staying on in the business, either in a behind-the-scenes capacity, or something more, (2) establishing a clear departure date or (3) devising a plan to phase out of the business.

Many parents find it easier to hold back on such a decision until the work relationship with the next generation has been solidified. Discuss it together, but do not be too hasty about arriving at a final decision, because you will discover things about each other—and yourself—as you work together.

In one well-publicized, and quite disastrous, succession, the uncle of two nephew-successors discovered that his decision to make the transfer of power had been premature. He gave the two boys "a little more authority and a little more expansion and a little more salary" than he thought they were ready for or deserved, because he thought that by doing so, they would appreciate the business more quickly. Instead, inventory and cash-flow problems rapidly began to occur, the uncle tried to take back the control he had given and a big family battle ensued. Obviously, it would have been wiser to have given over less in the beginning to see how it would go.

Barring illness or infirmity, proceed slowly and give yourself plenty of time to explore your changing roles. At the same time that parents are helping groom successors for their crucial jobs, they should also be thinking about what they want to do once they've stepped aside as the top managers in the firm, and ask themselves questions such as: "How much time do I really want to spend at work?" "If I stay, what new role will I assume?" "If I leave, do I plan a cutoff date, or phase out?" "And how will I use my time?"

The parent is the only one who can make such choices and, of course, in a family business, can do whatever he or she wants. Let's explore the options further, beginning with my own personal preference.

Staying on in the Business

As long as the elder member of the family remains healthy and in good physical shape, he or she should not really ever think of retiring from the business, in spite of the fact that the children in the business may be running it very well. Retirement, to my way of thinking, is the surest way of shortening the span of the rest of your life. I feel that even coming in a few hours a day is important. Keep active and, as George Burns says, "Get up and out of bed as soon as you awaken every day—don't hang around in bed."

So if this never-retiring route is for you (and I hope it is), let your children in business know that you do not intend to retire—that you may intend to give over the reins of the business to them, but you will stay on and work because that is what keeps you young.

To my way of thinking, phasing out of a business should only mean that you will be less involved with daily activities while you will still have knowledge of everything that is going on. At that point, you may wish to function as a senior adviser, offering advice when and if the children ask you for it or when, in your opinion, something is not being handled correctly.

In some families, the presence of the older generation at the time when everyone else is in place and running the show can hold back the forward momentum of the office. You'll know if that's the case. However, if you are one of those parents who has no problem ceding your authority and finding some peripheral project or area in the office in which to work, staying on may be the right approach for you.

"If I wanted to quit working now, I could quit working but I wouldn't be as happy not working," is how one father describes his situation.

"He's basically relinquished the day-to-day operation to us," is how one son describes his father's role, "and he is handling the more corporate areas. It's a big help."

For some parents, staying on is a golden opportunity to concentrate on areas of work they love best, but never before had the time for. They may even discover they have hidden talents where they never expected to find them, as happened in one case where the plan for succession involved growth through franchising. The son took over as top manager of the business, and the father, an endless source of knowledge of the business, went off to train those who would run the new outlets, offering them a level of excellence and pride of ownership that only he could impart. Sharing his wisdom and enthusiasm, this founder found a new role in the business as a gifted teacher.

If staying on in the business is my recommendation, it's not the only way of doing things once the next generation is ready to take over, so let's look at some of the other options.

Establishing a Departure Date

This has got to be a mutual decision; would-be successors must be as comfortable with this approach as you are. "They don't want me to go right now," explained one father, just as his daughter exclaimed in no uncertain terms, "He *couldn't* walk out right now!"

In another situation, both father and daughter are pretty much in agreement as to how succession will occur. "I have come to the conclusion," explains the father, "that I have to physically kind of disappear. I sense that people are coming to me before making decisions, that they don't move until I tell them what to do. Probably my fault, and I'm saying that my daughter would be tougher and better running this business than I am." Like several other parents interviewed for this book, he's also prepared to go off and try a whole new career. His daughter, meanwhile, is preparing herself for the inevitable. "It's going to be a whole other thing when Dad leaves," she says. "I think it's wonderful, and I think it's great that he's willing to leave, but at the same time, it's a real mixture. He does such a great job, he's been a wonderful boss, not because I'm the daughter, but I think a lot of people in the company agree with me. So while I'm really glad he's leaving, at the same time I feel all this stress, knowing I have to fit in his shoes, but

I'd rather do it now. It's kind of strange. I'm scared, but I can't wait."

Often it is a good idea to plan for a definite departure date and to stick to it. If you suspect that your children will call on their own resources and rise to the occasion more rapidly when you are gone, this might be the best approach to take in planning your departure. Explains one son, "My parents are years from hanging it up. They are very young-at-heart people, so they're not ready for Florida and the wheelchair sort of thing. But come August, they will both officially be going off to pursue other areas of life besides the business."

A departure date can be timed with some other significant change taking place. Having groomed his forty-eight-year-old son-in-law successor, primed his daughters for the transition and become more or less satisfied with the setup he has initiated for their taking over, one founder of a very large and successful corporation in the Midwest plans to leave when his whole operation is moved to larger headquarters. "My biggest fear is that my father will find the idea of retirement so hard to take that he'll delay, and we won't have time to work together as his successors," explains one of the daughters. "It's important that we get a chance to practice our new roles while he's still here."

Phasing Out of the Business

In a sense, phasing out provides a perfect opportunity to practice new roles in each other's absence before the final change is made. How can you accomplish this?

■ **Take vacations.**

"I'm planning a lot of vacations!" exclaims one delighted father. "I've got about three or four vacations planned. And I'll add on a few days to some of my weekends."

■ **In your absence, delegate total authority to your successor.**

While helpful in preparing successors for the absence of a parent, keep in mind that trips and vacations can only go so far if the authority of the older generation is still very much in place. Outside contacts and nonfamily members particularly feel this. Thus, to make the most of vacations and other planned absences, successors must clearly and very publicly be given authority to make their own decisions.

■ **Cultivate outside interests and activities.**

"Well, he doesn't play golf," says one son, describing his father. "He plays at being the mayor of his town." Work, obviously, is not everything for this multitalented parent.

Staying on, phasing out, leaving or whatever the final choice agreed upon, both you and your successor will benefit from practicing new roles while you both are still around. Your ultimate goal of succession is to put the business in the capable hands of family members. You may be happy to be out of it to enjoy new pursuits, to watch with infinite satisfaction the next generation as they continue the success of the business you have bequeathed to them. Or you may want to stay on in a less central, but key, position—ceding top authority and concentrating on areas of work you have never had the time or opportunity to dive into. It's up to you to decide.

MONKEY WRENCHES

Despite all good intentions, succession plans can take unexpected turns. Let's look at some of the most common ones.

A change of heart.

Suppose, with all good intentions, you make a plan to end or gradually phase out your presence in the office, but in doing so, change your mind and want to come back. It's a sign you are probably just not ready or able to give up your work. You should have every right to change your mind.

"My father goes on vacation to Florida," says one son. "He signs off for the month of February. Two years in a row, he has come back well before the month is up. He's bored. He wants to come back and work."

"And while he's not supposed to be in here Wednesdays because he plays bridge," the son continues, "more often than not he'll walk into the office at nine o'clock in the morning. 'Dad, what are you doing here?' I'll say. 'Well, I'm not playing bridge until twelve o'clock,' he answers."

You should talk about the possibility of a change of heart in advance. It should be a parent's prerogative to stay on, provided you have made a clear transfer of authority to your successor, announced it publicly and shown that you can live with the consequent change in your status.

Illness, death or some other sudden departure of a parent.

These things happen. How such a crisis affects the business depends on how far into succession planning you are when the unexpected occurs. Hopefully, at the very least, you will have chosen the line of succession and designated a successor. More often than not, personal crises accelerate the process of maturity, and many children rise to the occasion and competently assume the responsibilities involved in taking on leadership.

Since no one can know the future, if you care about your business at all, it behooves you to take the bull by the horns and confront the issue of succession as soon as possible. It's never too early to communicate enthusiasm for your work to your children, and while you cannot force them to fulfill your dream of having them take over, you can certainly share your wishes with them at the time they begin formulating career plans.

Recognition that children/successors are not competent or suited to take over the business.

Again, it can happen. And the sooner everyone faces up to such a possibility, the better. Sometimes children make this discovery and choose to leave; other times, with the fate of the business at stake, it falls on someone else (preferably not the parent) to make the determination and openly discuss it with the child. It's never easy, but handled with sensitivity and care, without blame or criticism, it can be done. There are two essential requirements for handling such a situation:

First, be prepared with performance reviews of all employees, to help diffuse attention from one incompetent individual.

Second, the firing should be done by someone outside the family. If necessary, call a consultant in to do an overall evaluation of management and make the necessary determination.

Outsiders seeking to buy out or control the company.

More and more frequently, this is one of the toughest challenges for families who have envisioned keeping control of their business.

Should outsiders "make you an offer you can't refuse," the first line of action is for all family members to privately but openly discuss the matter. Weigh all factors carefully and give your opinions. No matter where you are in the succession process, be prepared to defer the final decision about how to proceed to the family members slated to take over.

Succession is a process. The earlier and more carefully it is planned, the more smoothly it will go.

How do families feel—at the brink of, or after, this final stage of succession?

Says one son, "Once in a while I find myself fighting and fighting and fighting, and I get my folks to agree with me, or not disagree, and I make my point and then later on when I'm alone, I get scared. 'Jees, I talked them into that!'

I tell myself. 'Maybe it was the wrong decision! Maybe I should have walked away and said okay!' " Despite his reservations, it bodes well for the future that he is unafraid to make his own decisions and stand behind them.

Says one daughter, whose father has given her total decision-making authority, but who is definitely staying on, "He's always here. Even when he's not here, he's here. If I go away, I go away. If he goes away, he can think almost more clearly about what's happening here, it seems. He's focused on it. Thinking of every little detail."

Wrap-up and Review

This book has focused on one of many aspects that contribute to the success of a family business—achieving a harmonious work relationship that encourages success in the business. While every business profits from the positive interactions of its employees, pooling their talents and pulling together as a team toward increased success, most businesses manage to survive and may even thrive in spite of the fighting that might take place among key employees and managers. While this kind of a situation doesn't make for a pleasant atmosphere, in a nonfamily business you can lock up the office at the end of each day, return home to the ones you love and leave the problems behind. If things are going badly between you and your employees, chances are that even with possible firings, you can go to sleep at night knowing the situation will eventually improve. Not so in a family business. Harmony among key employees—people you have grown up with, nurtured and depended on for emotional support—counts for every measure of success. When the relationships between immediate family members and relatives are going well in the office, the benefits spill over into family life on a very personal level. Work becomes a special joy, the pride and pleasure in each accomplishment deeper and more satisfying than ever. On the other hand, when family connections are terrible at work, they can often cause irreparable personal distress.

The previous ten chapters have presented typical areas and issues in a family business where maintaining harmony is a particularly important objective. The topics have been discussed here in a loose, chronological order beginning with the first thoughts of bringing family members in, all the way through to the succession stage. In reality, of course, the issues are not always going to present themselves in such a neat, orderly fashion. However, it seemed a viable structure for the book to arrange the subject matter this way, in hopes that families at any stage of working together could quickly find and make the most of what others have done to keep their close relationships intact when in difficult situations.

Thanks to the generous cooperation and input of the families who contributed their ideas and insights, I hope you have found pearls of applicable wisdom strung across every page of this book. Each success, each style of coping is different, but patterns for keeping together in the workplace do emerge. Remarks, anecdotes and words of advice so eagerly shared in interviews for the book indeed began to echo one another. In review, they also provide a perfect departure point for readers who are eager to make the best of their family connections. Taken from the text, here is a collective list of basic principles and personal philosophies that families depend on for keeping harmony in their family businesses.

BASIC PRINCIPLES FOR FAMILY HARMONY ON THE JOB

- Really love the business. Truly enjoy it.

- Really love being together. You must connect well at home before you consider working together in the office.

- If your dream is to bring family into the business, tell them. Talk openly about the possibilities. Bring the subject up as soon as you know this is what you want. Don't hold back.

- Be sure there is a mutual willingness to work together. If the ability is there, let the younger generation make the final choice to come in.

- Take the view that working together is an opportunity, not an obligation.

- Pinpoint your motives for working together; confirm that they are mutually beneficial ones for the business and for yourselves.

- Treat each other as valued partners in the business.

- Respect all the years of success and hard work that went before you entered the family business, and the good ideas each member of the family will generate in the years to come.

- Give the space and freedom necessary for a new generation to find its own niche, its own style of doing business.

- Divide responsibilities fairly, according to talents.

■ Treat family members as who they are, not who you wish they would be.

■ Do not take away responsibilities once they have been delegated.

■ Listen to each other—really listen.

■ Solicit opinions. Common sense knows no age and often provides the most obvious solutions.

■ Keep politics, particularly autocracy, out of the family business.

■ Openly and mutually establish a trial basis for working together, with competence the one and only criterion.

■ Distance personal emotions from business decisions. In the office, put the business first.

■ Confront conflicts, work to resolve them and then let them go.

■ Avoid taking sides when others in the family fight. Try to let them work together to resolve their conflict, but be willing to give an opinion if it is called for.

■ Show no favoritism among family members in the firm.

■ Treat relatives as fair job candidates first, family second.

■ Use your social relationship with family outside the office as a barometer of how it's going inside the office. If things feel strained, openly determine whether it is a personal matter or a business matter.

■ Back off from personal matters if distance is preferred, but offer to discuss them too.

■ Give space to let family members develop a personal life.

■ Pick your battles carefully.

■ Keep and cultivate a sense of humor.

■ Admit when you are wrong.

■ Be flexible, open to change and open to criticism.

■ Welcome criticism and suggestions for improving work style.

■ Communicate on everything. Keep each other up-to-date on what's going on.

■ Be open and willing to ask questions, and to answer them.

■ Give honest compliments to each other. Seek out areas and actions to compliment.

■ Champion each other's success in the business. Support each other.

■ Determine that your mutual goals for the business—the big picture—are compatible.

■ Do not expect perfection. There is no such thing.

■ Do not set unrealistic goals for family members that you would not set for others.

■ Treat family with the same respect and trust that you do other valued employees.

■ Treat nonfamily employees as you would family.

■ Keep your temper in check.

■ Avoid blaming each other for making mistakes. Ask not what you did wrong, but what you can do to make it right.

■ Don't try to change each other's work habits if the business is thriving.

■ Forget about searching out each other's faults; search for and acknowledge each other's strengths.

■ Be open with trusted nonfamily members about the future and where they stand in the company.

■ Keep your privileges, but let your offspring or the younger generation know they too will earn them someday.

■ Call on trusted nonfamily to help resolve business debates and conflicts. The best case presented, in terms of being good for the business, is the one that should be implemented.

■ Hold no grudges.

■ Put more value on intelligence than on age.

■ Plan together for the future well-being of the business—ideally, when family is first coming in. Establish a financial plan for succession, and make it clear to everyone in the firm what the line of succession will be.